VACATION HOUSES

VACATION

BETSY & HUBBARD COBB

HOUSES

WHAT YOU SHOULD KNOW BEFORE YOU BUY OR BUILD

GALAHAD BOOKS · NEW YORK CITY

Library of Congress Catalog Card Number: 74-16557
ISBN 0-88365-274-9
Design by Bob Antler
Printed in the United States of America
Published by arrangement with The Dial Press

CONTENTS

v

ILLUSTRATIONS

The authors have endeavored to include both attractive and representative examples of vacation houses and vacation developments, but the inclusion thereof in no way constitutes an endorsement of house plans, buildings, or developments.

VACATION HOUSES

1 YOU, TOO, CAN HAVE A VACATION HOUSE— IF YOU HURRY

It is quite possible that the 1970s will go down in history as the decade of the Great Land Grab. This time, the mining or timber or oil interests won't be doing all the grabbing. Instead, millions of ordinary Americans, for any one of several reasons, have an almost desperate desire to own a piece of land on which to have a home away from home. A vacation home is the New American Dream.

Some of these land-hungry Americans will buy older houses (if they can find them) and remodel them; some will build their vacation homes themselves; others will buy leisure homes in planned vacation communities; still others will watch, round-eyed, while "instant" houses of all varieties are unloaded on their property from giant flatbed trucks. All will feel a deep satisfaction and a sense that something like Salvation is just around the corner.

Starting in the 1960s, the trend toward second homes accelerated so rapidly that by 1967 the U.S. Bureau of the Census decided to see what it was all about, and that year made the first national census of this hitherto unnoted and unexplored manifestation of an apparent national need to get back to the land —or the sea. The census report was published two years later,

3

in 1969, and it is still the most detailed information available. It showed that 1,700,000 second homes were already in existence and that approximately 425,000 of these homes had been built during the seven and a half years from January 1960 to April 1967—a rate of about 60,000 second homes a year. And the pace was accelerating. It still is. By late 1971, almost two million American families were leading double lives—one in their primary near-the-job home and the other in their vacation house away from home. There still may not be a chicken in every pot, a roof over every head, a second car in every garage, but according to a lot of the smart money, by 1975 there will be a second home for some 200,000 American families a year!

Two hundred thousand vacation houses going up every year. Heaven help the lakes, the ocean, the mountains and the desert, the wild animals and birds, the brooks and the rivers. Heaven help us all if we build this many houses every year in the same unthinking, unplanned, mismanaged, and often ruthless manner as we have in the past. Industry has not been the sole offender in the ruin of so many thousands of square miles of our best natural recreational areas. A good deal of acreage has been ruined by vacation houses.

Fortunately, some areas are taking steps to preserve the environment in their remaining recreational areas while still making sites available for vacation houses. Vermont, usually associated with going along with Maine, has taken a lead in this field and passed some tough laws governing the use of land and its development. Under one law, in towns without permanent zoning to regulate growth, all land development of more than *one* acre has to be passed by the District Environmental Commission, and even in towns with permanent zoning, all developments of more than *ten* acres must be certified by the same commission. Good for Vermont! Like everything else American, it wants to grow, "But," says the new law, "haphazard, poorly planned growth, whether it be highway, strip development, poorly sited vacation homes or industrial sprawl, cannot be allowed to dominate our growth in 1970."

As more states become aware of what's going on, as more

people become concerned about what's happening to the remaining undeveloped land, more such laws will pass. They will probably make it more difficult and more expensive to have a vacation house—which may work a hardship on some—but we will be able to pass on to our children something more than a great recreational slum.

The time is running out when ownership of land gives you the right to use it in any fashion you wish. There are still plenty of areas where you can buy a piece of land, put a shack on it, and let the sewage from it drain into a nearby lake or river. And there are still places where you can cover a piece of land with a lot of little rental cabins or put in a huge vacation development that transforms a local beach or lakeshore into a miniature Coney Island on the Fourth of July, but these places are becoming harder and harder to find. And, hopefully, it won't be too long before they can't be found at all.

There will be little room in the future for today's popular concept of a vacation house—an attractive single-family dwelling on its own acre or so of land by the edge of a lake, on the shore, or in the mountains. It can't be like this if you are talking about anything close to 200,000 vacation units a year. In fact, the familiar vacation house is already beginning to fade out of the picture because there simply isn't that much land with natural recreational facilities near heavily populated centers. Or, at least, land that the average family can afford to buy and build on.

The trend will be toward more planned vacation communities, for it will be the large developers who will have the resources to buy and develop large tracts of land in compliance with local and state regulations. And it will be only these big outfits who can afford to create recreational facilities where no natural ones exist. Already we find developers putting in manmade lakes and even ski slopes covered with artificial snow. Golf has become such a popular form of recreation—almost a compulsion with some—that an 18-hole course can in itself make a vacation community a paradise for many men, women, and even their children.

There are going to be fewer and fewer conventionally built vacation houses. The trend will be toward manufactured units of one kind or another—precut, prefab, or modular, and to the condominium type of dwelling.

And like everything else, vacation living is going to become more conformist. There will be less room for individual expression not only in the design of the house but in the way of life. The old man will be hard put to find a place where he can feel comfortable spending his weekend lolling in the front-yard hammock in his undershirt, sipping beer and listening to the ballgame, or where the old lady can wear sloppy jeans and let the household chores pile up while she reads *War and Peace.*

Vacation house sites are going to get more and more expensive. This is probably true with everything, but it is especially true of vacation land. It is going to cost the developer more to put together a vacation community that complies with state and local regulations, and it's going to cost him more to put in all the amenities that people demand in a vacation community. And this means more expensive houses, for there must be some relationship between the cost of the house and the cost of the land. And the developer still has to make his profit.

If you are toying with the idea of getting a vacation house, today is as good a time as any. No matter how you slice it, by tomorrow it's going to be harder to find what you want, and it will cost you more as well.

WHAT DO YOU WANT FROM A VACATION PLACE?

It wasn't so many years ago when this would have been a foolish question. The answer was obvious: "A place to spend our vacation, dummy."

Those were the simple times. A vacation house was strictly a summer place; whether costly or inexpensive, most such houses were on the primitive side with a minimum of plumbing, kitchen equipment, and similar conveniences. They were called "cottages" or "camps" and were delightfully easy to maintain. A family moved into their vacation house after school was out in June and shut it up on Labor Day. If it wasn't too far away and the train service was good, Dad would come up on weekends, as well as for his two-week vacation. If the place was near the water, the family could swim, boat, or fish. If it wasn't near the water, the kids played in the fields or woods and Mom and Dad sat on the screened porch and read. A family picnic was a big event.

Those days are gone forever, and the whole concept of vacation houses has changed. In fact, today they are as often called "leisure homes" as "vacation houses" but for this book we'll stick to the old-fashioned title.

The popular concept of today's vacation house has as much in common with the vacation house of yesterday as a 747 jetliner has with the old DC–3. It is a second home with all the equipment and conveniences found in a typical year-round dwelling.

Vacation houses represent different things to different people. To some they remain the place to get away on vacations and weekends from the noise and confusion of the cities. Just a nice quiet place to relax and breathe fresh clean air—more or less. But to others they are a place to play—where the action is. You will find vacation areas designed for those who love to ski, to boat, to fish, to swim, to golf, to play tennis, to horseback ride, or just to have a busy social life. For more and more people a vacation house is the place where they hope eventually to live year round—if they can find a way to earn a living; for others it is the place that will become their retirement home.

So before you begin looking for a vacation house, decide pretty much what you want from it, both now and in the future, because this is going to influence where you look and what you look for.

If what you are after is nothing more than the old-fashioned kind of vacation house—a place to relax on weekends and during the summer vacation—distance from your year-round home is a primary consideration. Past experience on the part of many has pretty well proved that anything beyond a three-hour drive from home base becomes a problem for weekends, especially if there are small children in the family. And by three hours we mean a three-hour drive on Friday and Sunday nights in bumper-to-bumper traffic. It would be lovely if we could get back and forth to our vacation homes by train as our parents and grandparents did, but with today's trains, this is usually close to impossible. Some areas may have good bus service, and there are always planes, but that kind of travel becomes an expensive proposition. For most of us, a car trip is the only way to reach our vacation house.

How much of the year do you plan to use the place? During the summer months, the idea of spending winter weekends and holidays at the vacation house can be very appealing, but winter often brings a change of heart. The children have homework to do and extracurricular activities. There are social engagements and things to attend to around the main house. The roads may be covered with ice and snow. There is not much point in spending the extra money to build or buy a year-round vacation house and maintain it all winter long if you are going to use it only in mild weather. But if you really do plan to use the place the year round, choose a house in a neighborhood where there are other year-round people. There is nothing quite as lonely or bleak as spending a winter weekend surrounded by dark and deserted summer houses.

If there are children in the family, their recreational requirements need consideration. Adults can sometimes be quite happy spending a quiet relaxing weekend doing nothing in particular, but this isn't usually true of children. They like outside companionship and something to do—swimming, sailing, bike riding. Unless there are other young people around and some nearby recreational facilities, the kids are either going to be miserable, or some member of the family is going to spend a lot of time chauffering them from one activity to the next.

Your chances of finding a suitable building site in a good environment at a reasonable price, and within three hours' drive from an urban center, can be rather remote. If that's your situation, perhaps your best bet is to look for an existing house or structure that can be fixed up at reasonable cost. You should be prepared to check out every community within three hours' driving time from your home. And don't neglect the most obvious ones simply because you feel they will be far too expensive. Every now and then something turns up in these areas at bargain prices. It may be a structure on an estate that is being broken up, or it may be a large white elephant. Something of this sort can be a good deal if you've got some friends who would like to come in with you and the local zoning regulations allow two-family houses.

And don't pass up some of the relatively small planned vacation communities you may find in your general area. These are the places where you might still find a building site or an existing house that will suit your purse and your needs.

A place to play.   More and more families today are looking for a vacation house as primarily a place to play—to do their thing. If this is what you are after, you will look where they have the facilities you require. It's not too difficult to find facilities for golf, tennis, swimming, and even boating near your year-round home, either in a planned community or in an area where you might buy or build, but if you are a ski nut, or a deep-sea fisherman, or love saltwater sailing, obviously you go where there are mountains and snow, or salt water.

For the family looking for a place to play, the best choice, unless you are very rich, is a planned vacation community. Only this kind of place can offer a wide assortment of recreational facilities or specialized facilities such as skiing or saltwater sailing at a reasonable cost. More detailed information on these communities is given later on in this chapter and in Chapter 23, "Planned Vacation Communities."

A place to live and work.   If you are getting sick and tired of hectic city life or the dull routine of the suburbs, the right vacation house in the right community can become the nucleus of a year-round home where you can not only live but also earn your living. This approach isn't restricted to those few artists and writers who can presumably live almost anywhere and still earn a living. You will find salesmen, accountants, lawyers, clerks, doctors, and even bankers who have started with a vacation house and eventually found a way to live in and enjoy it all year round and still make a pleasant income. Some of them have continued in their original professions. We know a man in the wholesale lumber business who has found a way to run his business by telephone from his condominium apartment in a planned vacation community in California. Another acquaintance—an attorney—switched from a large New York firm to a small one in New England. Others have made more drastic changes in the way they earn a living. For example, an advertising executive is now the sales manager of a vacation community, and a former magazine art director has opened an art gallery near what was originally his summer place.

It's a lot easier to find a way to earn a living in a small community—assuming that it's the right community for you— if you start off with a vacation house there. Having a vacation house for a few years gives you the opportunity to get to know the area and your neighbors and to decide if this is really the sort of life you will enjoy the year round. It also gives you a chance to explore fully the opportunities for earning a living, so that when and if you make the switch, you'll land on your feet and not flounder around looking for some way to make an income and perhaps, out of desperation, settle for whatever comes along.

You should look for a house or land in or near a community with a year-round population. A typical summer resort is no good if what you need is a year-round job. Even if you can earn a living there, it can be a pretty dreary place in the off season. But a small year-round community within reasonable driving distance of larger centers can be ideal. Look for a community where zoning and other regulations will govern the rate and type of growth. You don't want to move into a community and find that in a few years it has lost exactly those qualities that made it appealing to you in the first place. If you have school-age children, you'll want to check out the quality of the schools and you'll also want to find out what lies ahead as far as real estate taxes go. Starting out with a vacation house will give you the time and opportunity to explore all these areas and see if this is really where you'd like to live.

A place to retire.   As far as we can learn, the three most important considerations in searching out a vacation place as an eventual retirement spot are the weather, the community, and the real estate tax—and we aren't at all sure what the order of importance should be.

Climate is certainly important, for as we get older we become less and less enchanted with cold, snow, and ice. Cold weather is not only a discomfort; a slip or fall on ice or snow can result in permanent disability. Cold is also expensive. You have to buy fuel to heat the house and warm clothing for yourself, and you have to remain indoors a good deal of the time. There are, of course, plenty of older people who wouldn't move from their snug little homes in northern Maine, North Dakota, or Minnesota—but plenty of others might head for warmer climes if given the chance. So, generally speaking, if you are looking for a vacation house that will eventually become a retirement place, you'll look for one in the milder climates— and that means Florida, southern California, New Mexico, Arizona, and areas along the Gulf coast.

Many people who retire in areas that have less extreme winters hope to find communities made up of people more or less their own age and with similar backgrounds. It's harder to make new friends as one grows older—and starting off with people with whom one has a lot in common makes the job easier. Since it's foolish to categorize a whole segment of the population merely on the basis of age, it is also necessary to mention that plenty of older people do not want to live in a community composed almost entirely of their own generation. As one friend of ours said, "I'd feel as though I'd been consigned to an elephant's graveyard, just standing around ready to die." This lady—and many others like her—prefers a nice mixture of people and ages—young, old, middle-aged—including dogs and cats.

There is one point on which most retirees, and others who live on fixed incomes do agree, however, and that is the subject of taxes, especially real estate taxes. With their earning power gone, and having to make do on a fixed income, they don't particularly like the idea of subsidizing a great many local improvements such as schools, sewage treatment plants, or a bigger and better town hall. So if money is a problem, better keep away from communities that are growing by leaps and bounds. Even if the taxes are low to start with, as more families move in, more facilities will be needed and taxes will go up.

It's not always easy to find a vacation area close at hand that meets the three basic requirements—mild climate, people with the same background, and a stable tax setup. What many have done is to buy a vacation house in an area they like, use it during their vacation period, and rent it to someone else for the rest of the year. Assuming that you can do this, the income from rent can go a long way in helping to carry the house while you are not occupying it.

As you can see, your primary reason for wanting a vacation house is going to influence where you look and also, to some degree, the kind of house you buy or build.

WHAT KIND OF VACATION LIVING DO YOU WANT?

In addition to deciding what you really want from a vacation house, you also have to decide what sort of total environment you want. There are two basic approaches. One is the approach offered by a planned vacation community where natural and man-made environments have been combined to produce a total package. If you buy into such a community you share in both the pleasures and the pitfalls. The other approach is to buy your own parcel of land and create your own environment. Each course has its advantages and disadvantages. One will appeal to a certain kind of person while another couldn't see it for dust.

The primary advantages of planned communities are:

1. They can offer recreational facilities that might not otherwise be available to individuals building or buying on their own.

2. They often offer vacation housing—such as condominium apartments—at a price below what it would cost to buy or build a house in a comparable setting.

3. Because maintenance and other problems are handled by the community management group, they provide as carefree an approach to leisure living as you can get today—unless you are very rich.

4. In many areas, they may be the only way to have a vacation house because there isn't any land available.

5. You will have a greater sense of security in a community because it is restricted to property owners.

The primary disadvantages are:

1. You will often not be able to put up just any kind of house. The community will specify, to a degree at least, the style and minimum-size house that can be built.

2. You will have to conform to certain regulations of the community. If you wish to rent your place at some time, for example, the management may have the right to approve the tenant. You may not be able to have pets. The list of restrictions can be fairly long.

3. Because many of these communities are often quite removed from other areas and are more or less self-contained, your day-to-day associations will be with members of the same

community. For some people, that's just fine—for others it can be awful.

4. You are going to have to pay for all those facilities, for maintaining them and for all that "carefree living," and you have no way of knowing in advance how these charges will increase in the future.

The advantages of getting your own piece of land and building on it or buying an existing house are:

1. You can build or buy whatever kind of house you want as long as you meet local building and zoning regulations.

2. You can sell or rent the house to anyone.

3. You can create your own style of living, and you will not have to conform to the general style set by the community.

4. You will become a member of the community at large and not an isolated segment of it.

But there are also disadvantages to this approach.

1. It's difficult to find land or an existing house on or near recreational facilities, and even if you do find it, the cost is often more than most people can afford.

2. If you build or remodel you'll have countless decisions to make and problems related to construction to contend with.

3. You'll have to worry about maintenance, the security of the house when you are away, and all the usual problems that come up with owning a house.

4. You may be more isolated from people than you wish to be.

As a general rule, we have found that planned communities have their widest appeal to the fairly affluent middle-income group looking for such recreational facilities as riding, boating, golf, tennis, skiing, etc. These communities also appear to attract gregarious people who enjoy the company of others, usually others with similar interests and income. Because of the initial cost of the land and of buying or building a house, plus the yearly maintenance involved, you are less likely to find young families buying into the more elaborate communities. The families with young children are attracted to either those communities that cater to their needs and pocketbooks, or to the more loosely organized communities where planning is more spontaneous.

Whichever they choose, though, most people still want exactly what the ads for planned vacation communities describe: *Care-free Leisure Living.*

The anti-planned-community groups consist on the one hand of the less affluent and those at the high end of the vacation house economic scale on the other. This approach appeals to the budget-minded because with a piece of land at a reasonable price, they'll eventually be able to build on it, even if they build only a minimal house. Or perhaps they can find something they can remodel. It also appeals to the top of the line— the rich can afford to have exactly what they want where they want it. The houses built for this group are the ones that get the attention—the ones you see featured in magazines and newspapers—designed by architects, decorated by famous interior designers, and set overlooking the ocean or a flowing ski trail. That is the American Dream Vacation House. For $40,000 and up, excluding land, it can be yours too.

2 HOW MUCH CAN YOU AFFORD?

Any vacation house is going to cost money. The question is, how much money can *you* afford to pay? We yield to the impulse to paraphrase the Frog-Footman in *Alice in Wonderland* by saying, "Are you able to afford anything at all? That's the first question, you know." Well, chances are you can afford something—if only a shack or tent. Perhaps you can afford a lot more. But before you set your sights too high, there are a few facts of life you should know about vacation houses.

That American Dream Vacation House we've been discussing can be a very expensive proposition, regardless of whether it is custom-designed by an architect, built from stock plans, put up by a developer, or remodeled out of an old casket factory.

The beautifully designed kitchen to make cooking and entertaining a breeze, the central heating and air-conditioning systems to keep you cozy warm or cool, those spacious outdoor decks, the massive stone fireplace, the ample bathrooms, the vaulted ceiling in the living room, and the breathtaking view of the ocean, lake, ski slopes, or golf course—they cost like the very devil. In fact, it will cost you as much if not more per square foot to build, buy, or even remodel an old structure into this sort of place as it will to build a good year-round house. For

16

what you are actually building is not a vacation house but a second home, and though it might be slightly smaller in area than a year-round house, the cost will be more or less the same —about $25 a square foot for living space. At this rate even a modest-size American Dream Vacation House with 1,000 square feet will cost around $25,000. That, mind you, is without land. And prime vacation land can cost plenty—$10,000, $15,000, even $20,000 a lot or more.

Despite these discouraging statistics there are plenty of ways to get something for a lot less, if you know how. And that is the reason for this book—to show you how.

The first step is to decide how much money you can put into your project and then look for something that fits your budget. It takes two kinds of money to swing a vacation house. First, you need a certain amount of cash for a down payment. To buy a medium-price house, using conventional methods of financing, you may have to make a down payment that runs 30 to 40 percent of the total cost. If the house you want costs $20,000, you will have to put up between $6,000 and $8,000 in cash just to sit in the game. If you are going to build a vacation house, you will first need land to put it on, and even if you can get a loan to finance the purchase of the land, you will still have to make a down payment on the house. And whether you buy both house and land or a piece of land alone, you will need extra cash to cover the closing costs—maybe $500 or more.

Next, you are going to need money to keep the house after you have bought or built it. If you have to finance part of the cost, you'll need money every month of the year for X number of years to cover the payments on the interest and principal. You will also need money to pay real estate taxes and insurance. All these are fixed costs, and they apply whether you are staying in the house or have it shut down tight.

On top of the fixed costs you will have basic operating costs —charges for utilities, heat, telephone. These will vary somewhat depending on whether or not the house is occupied and on the climate. And don't forget maintenance. A good rule is to allow about 2 percent of the total cost of the house for yearly upkeep and repairs.

And you have to figure transportation—getting to and from the house. (Watch out for this one, especially on weekend houses, for it can add up to a lot of money fast.) You may, for example, have to buy a car or a second car in order to use your house. If so, your costs are not only the price of the car but also insurance, repair, and maintenance, plus gasoline and oil. If you are going to have to use other means of transportation such as train, plane, or ferryboat, figure these in.

To give you a better idea of exactly how much it takes to own a vacation house, let's itemize some of the basic costs on a house that cost $20,000. We'll assume you made a down payment of $8,000 and were able to get a 15-year mortgage loan at 8 percent interest—not a bad deal on a vacation house. Because the house is winterized and not too long a drive from home, you use it not only in the summer but also for weekends during the fall and early spring. Your expenses each month will run something like this:

1.	Mortgage payment	$112.96
2.	Insurance	9.30
3.	Real estate tax	21.00
4.	Gas & Electric	16.00
5.	Telephone	6.00
6.	Heat	10.00
7.	Transportation	12.00
8.	Maintenance—supplies and services	30.00
	Total	217.26

So you see, that rather modest little $20,000 place is going to cost more than $200 a month just to own, and that comes to a tidy sum yearly. We did not include the cost of furnishing the place, equipping it with pots and pans, or adding all the other essentials you'll need for comfortable living. We also didn't ask where the $8,000 for the down payment was going to come from.

There are other expenses you should take into account in budgeting for a vacation house. One of these is entertainment. In some areas this can be a very big item. If you buy a house in a community with an active cocktail circuit and you want to be one of the good guys, it's going to cost a good deal of money just for booze. And it's pretty hard to have a vacation house and not have friends for a weekend, and they can eat and drink away a good deal of money. There is also the matter of recreational equipment. If you have a place on or near the water you may find all sorts of reasons why you should own a boat. Or maybe the entire family will decide to take skiing or tennis lessons. You can drop a lot of money for recreational equipment, so better set aside a few bucks for it.

The above is not meant to scare you off from owning a vacation house but to help you think realistically about what kind of house you can actually afford to own and to maintain. Bankers and other lenders can tell you that a lot of people get in over their heads on vacation houses. They buy a more expensive place than they can afford. They don't really figure out the cost of ownership and the added expense of operating two establishments. And all of a sudden things catch up with them. The house they bought as a place for enjoyment and relaxation becomes a horror house of worry and anxiety. Frequently the house has to be sold—not always at a profit. Even if you can skate on financially thin ice, it's hard to have much fun in a place where every night you turn and toss worrying about how to pay the next installment on the mortgage or where to get the money for real estate taxes.

So figure out what you can comfortably afford to spend each month—twelve months a year—for a vacation house, and make the necessary adjustments to finance it. You may want to do what many others have done, and that is to reduce the cost of your year-round residence so you'll have more funds and time available for your vacation house. You may decide, for example, to move into a smaller and less expensive year-round house, or perhaps a condominium apartment, and make the vacation house your real "home base." Whatever you do, the point is to pick a vacation house that comfortably fits your budget.

If you are broke but don't mind roughing it, you can pick up an acre or so of land in some remote place—there are still a few attractive areas in the country where you can buy land for $100 or $200 an acre—and pitch a tent or build a shack on it with your own hands. You may have to reach your camp on foot, and it will lack modern conveniences, but if this is what you can afford, it's a lot better than nothing, and for some people, it's heaven. If you are very rich, you can commission an architect to design and build a real "conversation piece" for you for a couple of hundred thousand dollars, get it featured in a magazine, and set architectural critic Peter Blake screaming, "Harry K. Thaw! Where are you now that we really need you?" In between these two extremes you'll find a great variation in prices.

Here are some examples of what you can get in certain price ranges. These prices do *not* include the cost of land because this can run from $100 an acre to $25,000 or more per lot.

$500 to $1,000.   For this kind of money you can get a good tent with a wood floor that will accommodate up to six people, or you can build a minimum shelter yourself that will handle four people. It is essentially a temporary camp rather than a permanent home but you can't beat the price, which includes such essential equipment as a camp stove, ice chest, lanterns, chemical toilet. You can save the cost of buying land if you rent, but if you own the land, this camp can be a good place to live while you build a more permanent house.

$1,000 to $5,000.   This can get you started on a permanent vacation house. What you can actually get in this price range is a shell, either custom-built or pre-cut. Obviously, the more work you do yourself, the larger the unit you can afford. On the other hand, the smaller the house, the more complete it can be made in this price range. What you will start out with, of course, is still pretty much of a camp because at this price no

well, sewer system, inside plumbing, or electricity is included. But these can be added later when you can afford them, and in the meantime you'll have a good start on an honest-to-goodness vacation house of your own.

$5,000 to $10,000. If you are willing and able to settle for a mobile home, you can have a nice two-bedroom job along with water, septic system, and electricity for under $10,000. If you can do a good deal of the work yourself, you can take that shell in the $1,000–$5,000 range and finish the interior as well as adding plumbing and electricity. We estimate that the cost of a drilled well, pump, septic system, one bathroom, and electric wiring will cost around $3,000 if you have it all done for you. If you do some of it yourself, you can naturally save some money. Figure the fixtures, materials, and labor for one bathroom at around $1,000.

$10,000 to $15,000. If you keep your sights down and select a small house that can be put up complete for $10,000, the additional $5,000 will easily cover the cost of plumbing and wiring and leave a bit over to cover some of the unknowns. If $10,000 is your limit, you've got to figure on doing some of the work yourself. This is especially true if you want a house of a comfortable size that will be adequate for a family and not just a single person or a couple. In this price range you may also find some small but complete manufactured houses as well as some large and rather luxurious mobile homes.

$15,000 to $25,000. This is a dangerous price range. There's a lot available in the form of stick-built as well as manufactured homes but there seems to be a tendency to buy at the top of the line and not make provisions for any extra plumbing and wiring. Remember that each time another bathroom is added, your plumbing costs go up another $1,000 or so.

$25,000 to $35,000.   In this price range you may be able to swing buying an existing structure and remodeling it. There is also a good deal available in the smaller planned vacation communities as well as condominiums and smaller houses in some larger developments. If you are building on your own lot, you'll be able to get a comfortable and complete house if you don't make it too big or too fancy.

$35,000 and up.   You don't have much of a problem finding something in this price range if you don't get too greedy. For $35,000 you can have a well-designed, comfortable year-round vacation house. And you won't have to do any of the work on it yourself.

Don't feel too unhappy if you find that your budget won't begin to cover the cost of that American Dream Vacation House. A lot of other people are in the same boat. As a matter of fact, according to the latest census report, the median cost of a vacation house is below $8,000, and that means there are as many vacation houses that cost less than $8,000 as homes that cost more. And we know what kind of a vacation house you can get for $8,000.

This brings up an interesting question: who does own those lovely American Dream Vacation Houses? All sorts of people do, and they have one thing in common—a lot of money. Their vacation homes represent only a small fraction of the total houses in the country, but because they are the outstanding ones, the ones featured in newspapers and magazines, it's not too difficult to believe that everybody has similar homes. Well, they don't. Build the vacation house you can comfortably afford. It may never become a conversation piece, but it will be a pleasant and happy place for you and your family.

3 | BE SURE YOU HAVE AN ATTORNEY

Buying real estate is a tricky business. It doesn't matter what kind of property is involved—land you plan to improve yourself, land in a vacation community, an existing house, a condominium—it's tricky. It is essential when you buy real estate that you have a good attorney on your side. And you need him at the beginning, to *keep* you out of trouble, rather than later on, to *get* you out of trouble. Too many people sign papers and write checks and the next thing they know they've got a problem that even the best attorney can't solve.

Every real estate transaction starts off with an agreement of sale, which is a contract between the buyer and the seller. This spells out the details of the transaction and everything that follows is based on what is put down in this contract. Once you have signed the agreement of sale, you are legally bound by it. The smart thing to do, and something that far too many people don't do, is to consult an attorney *before* signing this contract.

So have an attorney and have him early in the game. Your best bet is to use a local attorney—someone familiar with local and state regulations regarding zoning, subdivisions, and building regulations. A local attorney who specializes in real

23

estate knows the names of the people to get vital information from, he knows his way around the town clerk's office where the property records are kept, and he probably knows something about the developer, the land, or even the house involved. Last year some friends of ours were interested in buying a piece of land for a vacation house. The price was very attractive and they called their attorney and asked if he happened to know that particular parcel and what did he think of the deal. He made a few phone calls and came back with the information that the area in which the house was situated had been rezoned to allow industry to move in and that an adjoining piece of land had already been purchased as a possible site for an oil refinery. Only someone who is familiar with an area can turn up this kind of information in a hurry. Also, a local attorney will be readily available when and if problems occur regarding the transfer of the property—and they often do occur.

If you already have your own attorney, he may be able to give you the name of a colleague who specializes in real estate in the area where you are buying. The local bank where you are getting a mortgage loan may also suggest someone, and real estate brokers can usually give you some names. Try to locate an attorney who is recommended by several persons. Just as in any other profession, all attorneys are not great, and some are awfully good but have certain failings. We know an excellent attorney who handles real estate, but he has a slight drinking problem, and when he's drunk he's not as quick as when he's sober. Another lawyer is so involved in state politics he can seldom be reached, and a third one is never in his office during the trout and hunting seasons. The attorney you choose doesn't have to be young or handsome or even very likable—just smart and sober and available.

An attorney can't do much for you, however, if you simply toss him an agreement-for-sale contract drawn up by the seller or his broker and ask if it's OK. Your lawyer should know what you expect of the property and what you plan to do with it. If you are buying a large parcel of land with the idea of selling some of it, tell him so. There may be local restrictions that prevent your doing this or make it financially impractical to do so. Or you may be buying an old summer cottage with the idea of fixing it up for year-round use in an area where zoning regulations prohibit making a year-round house out of a summer cottage. If you are buying a house from a private individual or from a developer, you should tell the attorney what you believe is included in the deal. He can then check to see if what you believe you are getting is really what you will get. He can do any and all of this only if you take the time to explain it.

An agreement of sale also spells out the financial aspects of the deal and when the title is to be transferred. If you are going to require a mortgage loan to purchase the property, there should be a clause in the agreement that states that if you are not able to get a satisfactory loan within a reasonable length of time, the deal is off and you get your down payment back.

Although checking out the agreement of sale or the sales contract may be the most important function of your attorney, many others things are almost as essential. He will make a title search of the property to be sure that it is free and clear and that you will have a clear title to it. If you are buying into a vacation community he can find out whether the developer has complied with all local regulations and determine insofar as possible what assurance there is that the community will be and will continue to be all you have been led to expect. He can save you headaches by finding out in advance whether or not at some future date you won't be slapped with heavy assessments to improve roads in the community so they will be acceptable to the local regulations, or to install a central sewage system because the individual house septic systems do not measure up to local regulations. And, finally, he will represent you at the closing when you receive title to the property, to make certain that your interests are protected and that the property involved is transferred in an orderly manner and to your satisfaction.

All this work is going to cost you some money, so find out in advance what the attorney's bill is going to be. Then it won't come as a surprise. Some attorneys have a fairly standard fee for an ordinary real estate transaction; some base their fee on the value of the property involved; and some charge by the number of hours they spend on the job. You'll find attorneys' fees can run from $100 to $500 or more.

4 FINANCING YOUR VACATION HOUSE

Whether you are buying, building, or remodeling, you will probably need financial help to swing your vacation house. There are several sources for money. Which source you use depends on how much you need, your financial situation, and what you intend to do. The most common ways to finance vacation houses are:

1. A mortgage loan
2. Refinancing the mortgage on your year-round house or taking out a second mortgage on it
3. Borrowing on life insurance policies
4. Taking out a personal loan
5. Financing the purchase through the seller: "taking back a mortgage"

MORTGAGE LOAN

This is your best bet when there is a sizable amount of money needed and you want to spread out

27

payments over a long period of time. You can get a mortgage loan to buy a house and the land that comes with it or to build a house on your own piece of land. You can sometimes get a mortgage loan to finance the land purchase alone. Mortgage loans can finance the purchase of an existing house to make necessary repairs and improvements on it. Mortgage loans are not available for houseboats, mobile homes, campers, and trailers because these are not considered real property and therefore must be financed through other means.

A mortgage loan for a vacation house is the same as one used to finance a year-round house, but the conditions of the loan are a good bit stiffer. On a year-round house intended as a primary residence, it's often possible to get a conventional loan of up to 90 percent of the cost and at a relatively low rate of interest. And the term of the loan can be up to to 35 years. On a vacation house you may have to make a *down payment* of up to 40 percent, and the term may be only 15 years. Also the interest rate will probably be higher than on your primary residence —anywhere from .5 to 1.5 percent more.

The reason for this difference in loan rates between vacation house and year-round house is that most bankers still consider a vacation house to be something of a luxury. The bank takes the attitude that if you have to borrow heavily to swing the deal, you're probably in over your head before you even start. And the stiff conditions will serve as an effective brake on your enthusiasm.

The best place to apply for a mortagage loan is in the area where you intend to buy—at a local bank or savings and loan association. A local outfit will be familiar with the area and property values. They can easily inspect the property to make a realistic appraisal, and as they have an interest in the growth of their community, they are more apt to underwrite a deal than an out-of-town institution concerned only with the financial aspects of the situation. Even so, you may have to shop around a bit to find an interested lender, and it may be that a bank where you are already known will be the one that comes through. It's a good idea to shop around in any case. Different banks have different policies on lending, and one may give you a better deal—a larger loan, lower interest, or a longer term—than another.

Banks are most interested in the more conventional type of vacation house—something that can be sold easily in the event you get into a financial bind and can't keep up the mortgage payments. They also look for property that has easy access to recreational facilities. Waterfront property is excellent if the water is suitable for swimming, boating, or fishing. Property near ski slopes or other natural or man-made recreational areas is also good. But if you want to borrow money to build a vacation place off in the woods, you'll have trouble getting money from the average banker.

When you apply for a mortgage loan, be prepared to answer a lot of questions. The lender will want your financial history, including current income and outstanding debts. He will make a pretty thorough credit check on you. He is also going to analyze your financial picture carefully to see if you can comfortably afford the vacation house you have in mind. For, regardless of how desirable the property may be, what is most important to the lender is your ability to keep up the mortgage payments. As one banker put it, "The borrower is our first line of defense—the property is secondary. We are in the business of lending money—not acquiring real estate."

If you have had to borrow money to buy the land on which you plan to build, the lender will probably turn you down. He'll also take a dim view of shelling out money if you are going to have to depend on the income you get from renting your place to pull you through. He will inquire as to where you are going to get the money for the down payment on whatever you are planning to buy. If you plan to swing this with another loan, he may turn you down. Bankers are not called hard-nosed businessmen for nothing.

The lender will also want to know a lot about the house you plan to buy or build. If it is an existing house, he will inspect it to see whether or not it requires major or immediate improvements or repairs. If you plan to buy and then remodel a structure, you should be able to show him what you plan to do and give him an estimate from a contractor on what it is going to cost. Also where you plan to get the money to pay for these repairs and improvements. If you are going to build, you should have plans and estimates on the total cost of construction. In the case of a do-it-yourself project, you should have a list of all the materials required plus what they will cost, including estimates on those portions of the work you won't be able to do yourself. You will also have to convince the lender that you are qualified to do any work you plan to do on your own. If you have had no previous experience in building, this won't be easy. It will certainly help matters if you can mention the names of friends or family who have had building experience and who will help you with the project. The average banker isn't against do-it-yourself projects, but chances are he's had a few unfortunate experiences with amateur builders who bit off a lot more than they could chew.

REFINANCING YOUR MORTGAGE

If you own a year-round house you can use it as security to raise money for the vacation house. One way to do this is to have the existing mortgage rewritten for a higher amount. This approach works, however, only if you started out with a relatively small mortgage or have paid back enough over the years to have acquired a sizable amount of equity in the property, or if property values have increased in your area or you have made major improvements in the house so that its true value has increased considerably.

The advantage of this method of financing is that once you have the money, you can do with it pretty much as you want. You can buy or build any sort of vacation house in any place that strikes your fancy—up to the limit of the amount of money you have. But there are some disadvantages, of course. If your original mortgage was taken out some years ago, you are going to have to shell out a lot more in interest when you refinance. For example, if the interest rate on your original mortgage was 5 percent, when you rewrite, the rate will probably be 7.5 percent or so. This will apply not only to the additional sum you get but also to the unpaid principal on the old mortgage, making your monthly payments considerably more. And last but not least, you are putting up your house as security for the vacation house. If you ever get in a financial jam and can't unload that vacation house, carrying your year-round house may become a problem.

SECOND MORTGAGES

If you own your own house you can take out a second mortgage on it to help pay for your vacation house. Second mortgages are short-term affairs—one to five years—and the interest rate is high—18 percent or more. The combination adds up to some pretty sizable monthly payments. The only time you should seriously consider taking out a second mortgage is when you are certain that the funds to pay it off will be available in the near future. For example, it might be better to take out a second mortgage than to sell securities at a time when you would incur a serious loss. Or you might take out a second mortage if you were waiting for an estate to be settled and would shortly have enough money to pay off the loan.

Second mortgages are also used by some vacation developers when a buyer does not have sufficient funds for a down payment. The second mortgage is written for the amount of the down payment, and a standard mortgage covers the balance. This is a fairly risky arrangement. The buyer has the combination of two payments for two mortgages, which can be a real financial drain. When you see advertisements for vacation houses requiring no down payment or as little as 10 percent, beware. If you need this sort of financing to handle a vacation house, you obviously can't afford it and shouldn't be kidding yourself that you can.

BORROW ON LIFE INSURANCE

If the loan value is adequate, this is a good way to help finance a vacation house. Life insurance loans go at a relatively low interest rate, you don't have to make monthly payments on them, and the life insurance company doesn't care what you do with the money. As with other kinds of loans, there are some disadvantages. As long as the loan is unpaid, the value of the insurance policy is reduced by the amount still to be repaid. There is also a tendency on the part of insurance borrowers to neglect to pay the yearly interest charge, and as this is then added to the amount of the loan, the amount owed keeps going up each year. But if you can pay the interest when it is due and make regular payments to reduce the principal, this type of loan is a good deal.

TAKE OUT A PERSONAL LOAN

This type of loan is offered by banks, credit unions, and other lending institutions for home improvements, car purchases, medical bills, and numerous worthwhile endeavors. If you own your own home or have a good credit rating, a personal loan isn't too difficult to get, and it can be a good way to swing a vacation house if you don't need too much money. The amount you can borrow depends, aside from your credit rating, on where you live. Some states allow you to borrow up to $10,000; others limit the amount to $5,000. The length of the loan can run from two to eight years depending on your requirements and state laws. Interest rates are higher than those on mortgage loans—around 12 percent—and as the life of the loan is relatively short, monthly payments are high. On the other hand, you do get the loan paid back in a hurry, and after that the vacation house is probably all yours free and clear.

Loans of this type are popular for financing the more modest types of vacation houses, for mobile homes, houseboats, campers and trailers, and especially for remodeling and do-it-yourself projects. Many families have financed quite extensive projects over a period of years with relatively small personal loans. As soon as one loan is paid up, they take out another and put the money into the house.

FINANCE THE PURCHASE THROUGH THE SELLER

Instead of going to a bank or mortgage lender for money to pay for the house, you may arrange with the seller to take back a mortgage for the amount you need, and then pay back the principal plus interest to him. Let's say you wanted to finance a $20,000 house and could make a down payment of $5,000. If the seller agreed, he would take back a mortgage for the balance—$15,000. It can be a convenient and handy arrangement if the seller will give you about the same rate of interest and length of term as you could get from a bank or similar lending institution. When you are buying from an individual owner, it may be a very feasible solution —especially if the owner is anxious to sell and would prefer a regular income from the property over a period of years rather than a lump sum, a big hunk of which might have to go for taxes.

You will find that many vacation community developments as well as dealers in mobile homes, shell homes, prefabs, and houseboats will also provide financing for the purchase of their property or units. Sometimes these arrangements are worked through a particular commerical lending institution and sometimes dealers or manufacturers have their own financial setups, the way some automobile manufacturers do. Purchasing property in this manner is similar to buying a car. The least expensive way to finance a car is through a regular bank. If you do your financing through a commerical credit house or through the dealer, you are going to pay more. Before you get too deep into financing a vacation house through a developer or dealer, find out the particulars. The Truth in Lending Bill requires that lenders tell you exactly what the interest on a loan is going to run. Find out in advance exactly what the monthly payments will be and what they will cover. Many lenders will add to the regular monthly payments additional sums to cover taxes and insurance on the property. Be sure you know what you are going to have to pay each month and what it covers.

5 LAND AND HOW TO IMPROVE IT

If your plan is to build your own vacation house rather than buy one already in existence, your first step is to find a suitable piece of land. Unless you already own some land—in which case the question becomes whether it is suitable to build on—your next move is to buy.

There are two ways to go about buying land. One is to look for an improved or partially improved lot or acre in a vacation community; the other is to hunt about and find a parcel of raw land you can improve and build on. More and more families today are buying home sites in developments—not necessarily because these communities offer their ideal of vacation living, but because they are unable to find suitable land anywhere else.

The big boom in vacation land has gone on for several years, and there is no reason to think it will not continue. You will find, for instance, that even in areas that are seven or eight hours' driving distance from urban centers, raw land is not only very expensive but also often impossible to buy at any price. Many factors have created this situation. Vacation house developers have purchased huge tracts of prime recreational land to improve and sell off in lots. Some of the largest corporations in the country are heavily involved in these vacation communities, and they have the financial muscle to buy not hundreds but thousands of acres of such land and to put in the necessary improvements so they can get a premium price for every lot. Private owners in these recreational areas are holding onto their property because each year they can see it increase in value. And even the owner of a small parcel of land —a farmer, for example—who might be interested in selling an acre or two, now sometimes finds that new restrictions aimed at preventing haphazard growth in the community make it impossible to do so. He must either sell all the land or none at all.

Also, not all land—even in prime recreational areas—is suitable for building. As you will learn later on in this chapter, soil conditions may prohibit installing a sewage system, or the below-ground water may not be fit to drink. Many thousands of square miles of land in this country can never be lived on, at least not until we make some rather startling technological improvements in the area of land development.

Finally, there is the cost of improving raw land, which can be a very expensive undertaking, especially if the land is in a remote area. Putting in a road, providing water, sewage disposal, and utilities, can run into thousands of dollars—often more than the private individual can afford. And more and more communities, even those in remote areas, are prohibiting building unless certain requirements such as adequate sewage disposal are met.

We don't mean to scare you off looking for a parcel of raw land outside a development, because it is possible to find—and even at a good price. But you must be prepared to travel a considerable distance, avoid the popular recreational areas, or perhaps settle for something less than ideal as the perfect site for a vacation house.

SHOPPING FOR RAW LAND

Raw land is the trickiest to buy, so we'll discuss it first before getting to the simpler matter of purchasing land in a vacation community. And when we speak of raw land, by the way, it means exactly that: no man-made improvements. There won't be roads into the building site, or a well, or sewage disposal, or utilities. Just a hunk of land.

The standard measurement for land is the acre, which is exactly 43,560 square feet. A building lot or plot is a fractional part of an acre—a quarter-, third-, half-, or three-quarter acre. The actual dimensions of the lot are usually given in feet—so many feet wide, so many deep. Raw land usually comes in large parcels, so it's sold and priced by the acre. Improved land is usually sold by the lot.

Occasionally you'll find land—both raw and improved— selling at so much a "front foot." This is usually prime water-front property, and the term means a strip of land one foot wide along the water running to a depth, usually, of 100 feet.

You will find a tremendous variation in the price of land even in the same general area. Land values are based on two primary considerations: location and the owner's desire to sell. You may find land in a remote section of a vacation area selling for a moderate price, while nearby land that is more accessible or on the waterfront or near good recreational facilities will cost an arm and a leg. Prices also vary according to the amount of land involved. You can generally pick up a large tract of land at less cost per lot or acre than you would pay for a single lot or acre of the same land. Many families have taken advantage of this wholesale pricing and have bought more land than they actually needed with the idea of selling off some of it to defray costs, or holding onto it as an investment. Another way to take advantage of a good price on a large tract of land is to make a group purchase—getting several friends to come in with you. Both these approaches are tricky. They are discussed in more detail in this chapter under the sections headed Land Invest-ment and Speculation and Making a Group Purchase. As a general rule, you are better off if you can find a piece of land suitable for your use alone.

About the best way to start shopping for land is through a real estate broker in an area that appeals to you. A local broker has a listing of much of the land that is on the market, and he can save you a lot of time and headaches by telling you if there is anything around that you can afford.

Not all land is offered for sale through a broker, of course. Many owners don't wish to pay the broker's commission, so they offer their land through ads in local newspapers, regional magazines, and even through *For Sale* signs along the road. And the fact that you talked to a broker doesn't mean you can't buy land directly from an owner. But since a broker can give you a good idea of land costs in the area, and other bits of useful information, it makes sense at least to start out with a broker. Also, working through a broker rather than on your own you are less likely to get stuck with a piece of submarginal land.

JUDGING LAND

To the land-hungry family, any piece of property may look attractive, but some land is suitable for home sites and some isn't. Some will cost more to improve. As soon as you find the piece of land that pleases you, begin to find out whether it will be practical and possible to build a vacation house on it. And the first thing to find out is whether or not the soil will support a septic system to handle the sewage and waste from the house. That's right! Don't worry yet about whether there is a nice site for the house, what kind of neighbors you may have, or the mileage to the nearest shopping center. First check out the soil for a septic system, because if you don't have the right kind of soil you may not be able to have a septic system, and if you don't have a septic system you may not be able to build a house on your own property.

States and local communities are finally getting very tough about septic systems. They have to. If the soil can't support septic systems, the resultant wastes will pollute not only the nearby land but also any wells, ponds, lakes, and rivers in the vicinity. And a lot of soils can't support a septic system. Clay won't, for example, nor will ledge rock. Certain types of soil called "hardpan" can be as dense as concrete, and a septic system in this soil is useless.

The only sure way to know if the soil can support a septic system is to have a percolation test made to determine the ability of the soil to absorb water. A test of this type involves boring holes in the ground, filling them with water, and noting the length of time it takes the surrounding soil to absorb the water. These tests are made by civil engineers and by licensed firms specializing in septic installations. You can get some advance information on the general quality of the soil in a given area from the county consultant for the Federal Soil Conservation Service—or from the county agent. Representatives of these two outfits are located at the county seat. You can also get a reading on general soil conditions from the local building inspector, zoning board, or planning commission. But don't take anybody's word that the soil is right for a septic system unless you have percolation tests that prove it.

Even if you don't plan to build on the land but merely to camp on it in a tent or camper, it's still important to make sure it will support a septic system. If it can't, you'll never be able to build on it, and what's more, you'll probably never be able to sell it, except to some other camper.

WATER SUPPLY

Water is another key factor in determining whether or not land is suitable to build and live on. And it's not just a matter of whether water is available but whether it is fit to use and drink. The water found in many lakes, ponds, and rivers is polluted, and even if your source of supply is pure at this stage of the game, you should have some assurance that it will continue to be pure. Even the water that comes from deep wells is not always fit to use. Some of it contains high concentrations of sulphur, iron, and other minerals. On the ocean it may be brackish. Another important factor is how much it will cost to dig or drill a well that will produce an adequate supply of water.

The cost of drilling a well is based on so many dollars a foot. Spring 1972 estimates run between $5.50 and $7.50 a foot, and if you strike an adequate supply at between 200 and 250 feet you can consider yourself lucky. Sometimes you aren't lucky. One family recently put down four wells, each more than 200 feet deep, before they struck water on the fifth. Total cost: $5,000 plus.

You can get general information on water resources in your area from some of the same people who know about septic systems—the county soils consultant, county agent, local building inspector, zoning and planning board. Tests can be made to see if water from a lake, pond, or river is pure enough to drink, but no one can guarantee it will stay that way. Past experience can be an indication of whether water from deep wells in your area is pure, or full of sulphur or other foreign material, but no one can predict how deep you'll have to drill to hit water. Not even the best well driller in the world can promise that he will hit water within a certain depth—if at all.

We have taken a lot of time to talk about septic systems and water because they are essential. The most beautiful piece of land in the country, available at a bargain price, isn't worth anything as far as a vacation house goes unless it can support a septic system and furnish an adequate supply of pure water.

THE SITE

The land should provide a suitable building site. Although it is possible to build a house on almost any piece of ground, the more uneven the terrain the more it's going to cost to put up a conventional house. If you are going to have an architect design a house for you (and if you are, it would certainly be wise to have him around when you select the land), an uneven or unconventional site may be OK and even desirable because he can design a house to fit the site. Also, an unconventional or difficult site will go for less than otherwise, you may be able to pay the architect's fee out of what you save on the cost of the land. If you are not going to use an architect, it is wise to stick to land that offers a good building site. A relatively flat piece of high ground is ideal. Avoid sites in a hollow or depression because they become soggy during wet weather; also steer clear of a proposed building site near a swamp. It is always a good idea to check a piece of land right after a heavy rain. You may find that a dirt road into the land becomes impassable, or that shallow ponds or swamps appear in otherwise perfectly dry areas.

A piece of land covered with rocks and boulders may be picturesque, but it raises the cost of putting in roads and building the house. The same holds for a heavily wooded piece of land. It costs money to take down trees and remove the stumps to make room for the house and road.

A good site should also lend itself to good orientation of the house. The best site allows the house to be set so that the long side with the large expanse of glass faces south. This is also the best side for outdoor decks and terraces. If the site is such that the living areas, glass areas, and outdoor areas face west, they will become uncomfortably warm in the afternoon until the sun goes down. If they face east they are pleasant in the morning but dark and shady all afternoon.

COST OF IMPROVEMENTS

When you buy raw land, the cost of basic improvements can become a major expense. Your basic improvements usually consist of the following:

1. Road through property to house site
2. Utilities: electricity and telephone
3. Water and sewage disposal

Roads. You are going to have to put in a road or driveway through your property from the nearest public thoroughfare to the building site. How much this will cost depends on how long the road has to be and what kind of terrain you have. Under ideal conditions, the minimum kind of dirt road costs about $2 a running foot. If you want a blacktop road, it costs around $6 a running foot for a road of average width. As soon as you get into uneven terrain or land with lots of boulders and trees to move out of the way, your costs go up. Even if there is an existing road into the site, it may not be adequate for your needs, especially during the time that the house is being built. A narrow trail may be all right for a Land Rover or Jeep, but it may be too small or uneven for a truck loaded with building materials or a well-drilling rig. Your best bet is to have a road contractor take a look at the property and give you a rough estimate on costs before you make the purchase.

Utilities. If you want electricity and telephone service, you'll also have to pay to have them brought in. Again your costs will be based on how far the site is from the nearest utility pole. You need a pole about every 200 feet across your property, and the cost of each pole plus wire runs about $100 installed. In other words, you can figure $1,000 for every mile. Many utility companies will allow you to finance this cost over a period of time, but it's still going to cost you money to get in power. (See Chapter 26, "Getting Along Without Electricity.") Costs for telephone lines are considerably less if poles have been put in for electricity. The cost here is about $50 for every mile of wire across your property.

Water. If your preliminary findings indicated that it will be practical to drill a well with the expectation of striking a good supply of water at a reasonable depth (six to eight gallons a minute should be adequate for the average family), you can figure that this system will run you about $2,000 complete with pump and tank. If you are able to get your water supply from a nearby lake, pond, or river, your costs will be much less. All you need then is a pump and storage tank, and the whole deal probably won't cost more than $200.

Septic system. Assuming the soil is suitable, a system costs from $400 to $700 installed.

These are the basic costs of improving land so that it is suitable to build and live on. Add them together and add them to the cost of raw land, and you'll see what it will actually cost before you even begin to build a house.

BUYING THE LAND

If you are happy with the piece of land in question, your next step is to buy it. Land is real estate, and real estate is a lot more complicated to buy and sell than a car, yacht, or diamond necklace. First of all, you have to sign a contract with the seller. This is called an agreement of sale, and it specifies the land involved, the price to be paid, and the time that the title is to be transferred. Before you sign this agreement, go over it with a lawyer—preferably a local one— to make sure the agreement jibes with your understanding of the deal. After you have signed the agreement you may have to make a down payment, and this amount should have been previously established and set down in the agreement.

Next, you need to have the title to the property checked out. This is done by your attorney. After he has made his search he can advise you of whether or not you will get a clear title or whether there are some encumbrances—unpaid taxes, easements, liens—that need to be cleared up. If there is some question as to boundaries, he may suggest a survey. Surveying is something you should try to get the seller to pay for since it costs a good deal of money. Even on a small building lot a survey might cost $200, and with several acres of rough or heavily wooded terrain the cost can be several thousands of dollars. If you are very anxious to buy, and the owner doesn't care one way or the other about selling, you'll either have to pay for the survey yourself or take a chance and do without it.

In any event, it is absolutely essential to have an attorney make a thorough search of the title. This is no do-it-yourself project, and it's not something that can be handled by a broker. Hire a lawyer and explain to him exactly how you want to use the land so that as he examines the records he can determine whether or not you can do what you have in mind. Once he has examined the title and found it in order, the next step is the closing, the point at which the money and title to the land are transferred. After that, the land is all yours.

Financing a land purchase.   Most land sales are made on a cash basis. One reason, of course, is that if you own a piece of land outright, it can often serve as the security for the loan to build a house. The other reason is that many lenders don't like to lend money on land—especially raw land. Too much risk is involved. Some banks will lend a certain amount toward the purchase of land, but usually only on prime land at a good price and for a short term—a few years at best. As is true for a house, the seller will sometimes take back a mortgage for his land. In either case, you'll have to come up with a pretty hefty down payment—maybe 40 or 50 percent of the selling price.

A lot of vacation land is sold and financed under what is called a "land sales contract" or "conditional sales contract." This is the kind of land you often see advertised in newspapers.

It usually sells for a few hundred dollars a lot. You are asked
to make a small down payment and then to pay off the balance
in small monthly payments. Aside from the fact that the interest rates you pay on this sort of deal are very high, you don't
have title to the land until you have made the final payment.
What you get is the use of the land until you have paid in full.
If you miss one payment, the land can revert back to the seller.
If you have built a house on it, that goes to the seller along with
the land. The seller will also get all the money you've paid in
as rent for the use of the land from the time you got involved
in the deal—even if you never set foot on the place.

Land investment and speculation.   In every vacation area
you can hear talk about people who bought some property a few
years ago for peanuts and then turned around and sold it for ten
or twenty times what it had cost. And if you are like most of us,
and hear enough of these tales, your mouth begins to water and
you decide that maybe you too can become one of those fortu-
nate ones who bought low and sold high.

There is no question that if you buy land or own a house in
an attractive vacation area, the property is going to increase in
value over the years. By and large this holds true of all real
estate. If the location should become more desirable because of
some special attraction such as the contruction of a nearby ski
tow, an artificial lake, a resort, a new Disney World, or some
similar attraction, the property value may increase even faster.
But, ordinarily, real estate values increase at a gradual rate
over the years. If you decide to sell in four, five, or ten years,
you'll no doubt make a nice profit. It will not, however, make
you a millionaire.

Buying a vacation house or vacation property, like buying
sound common stock, can be a good investment, but don't think
of it as anything more than that. And whatever you do, don't
speculate on vacation land unless you can afford to take a beat-
ing. Yes, some people make fortunes specializing in land—
some people always have—but they are the ones who know
what they are doing and have an inside track. They know

before anyone else which parcels are going to come on the market at an attractive price. They know what commercial developments are projected for certain areas, or that a certain tract is going to be turned into a state park, or that a river is going to be dammed to form a lake, or that a highway is projected that will make a certain parcel easily accessible. They also know which pieces of land can be developed and which can't, either because of terrain and soil conditions or because of state or local building regulations. In short, they know the territory and the people in charge, and you don't.

Making a group purchase. Buying land with others can often be a very good deal. As we pointed out earlier in this chapter, the larger the tract of land, the less you usually have to pay per acre or lot. So if you happen on a sizable chunk of land at a price that is good, but more than you can afford, consider getting some friends to go in with you. Even if they are not interested in a vacation house, they might want to go along merely as a good investment. And with such an arrangement, you'll not only be able to get some land for yourself, but there will be other savings. The cost of basic improvements to the land—building roads and bringing in utilities, for example—will be shared, thus reducing the cost to the individual.

But before you commit yourself to buying land with this in mind, check with the local planning and zoning commission to see if it can be handled as a group project, and if so, what the complications are. Communities are increasingly passing and enforcing regulations to control and restrict developments of every size. At one time such restrictions usually applied only to large developments, but now they often apply to any plan involving the construction of houses. You may find, for example, that you and your friends will have to put in the same kind of improvements—paved roads (that you would have to maintain) or a central sewage system—that a large developer would. And before you could even start, you'd have to have a topographical map made of the land and you would have to get reports from engineers as to soil conditions. You might go broke just paying for all the preliminary planning required to get approval to go ahead. If you can make a group purchase without too many difficulties, however, it's a good deal.

There are several ways to handle a group purchase. One is to divide the land equally among the several individuals involved. Another is to divide the land so that each member of the group owns a certain parcel and the remainder is held jointly by all the parties as common land. The latter is a good arrangement to have if the land includes something like a pond where everyone can swim, fish, or boat.

No matter which approach you use, be sure the entire transaction is handled on a businesslike basis. All the necessary papers should be drawn up by an attorney, and they should be inspected by each individual's attorney before they are signed. There should be some provision in the agreement to the effect that if one member decides to sell, the others get first refusal. This is especially important if part of the land is jointly held.

And naturally enough, there has to be a formal arrangement made for payment of taxes on all common property as well as the cost of maintenance—repair and upkeep of common roads, fixing the dam at the end of the lake, and maybe having some of the trees removed or treated with insect spray. You also must have a sensible arrangement covering any improvements on common property. Who decides what improvements are to be made, and how is the cost of the improvements to be shared?

Buying land in a vacation development. This is not quite as complicated as buying raw land, but you've still got to watch your step. State and local governments are getting tougher on developers to make certain that they comply with all regulations regarding density of population, sanitary facilities, ecology, and conservation. A good many of these developers do make an effort to comply with the letter of the law—and even go beyond it. But the fact remains that some developers don't. And there are cases where families who have built homes had to go to great expense to have a central sewage system installed in the community because the soil could not support separate septic systems, or who have found that the beautiful lake which was the reason for their buying has become polluted and is now useless for recreational purposes and a health hazard.

When you buy a building site in a vacation development, you have to consider the total development. No matter how attractive your piece of land may be, your enjoyment of it is going to depend on the development as a whole. You can't isolate your lot. Information on how to judge the quality and character of a development is covered in Chapter 23, "Planned Vacation Communities," so at this point we'll simply discuss a few vital aspects of the site itself.

Building sites in a development are laid out on a map or plat plan so that you can readily see the size of the lots in relation to each other, their location as to main roads, and recreational facilities. Lots are priced according to their size and location, the most expensive being those close to the prime recreational facilities such as a lake of golf course, or those with the best view. In many a vacation development you'll find a difference of tens of thousands of dollars between the golf or waterside site and the site back in the woods. Needless to say, the sites shown in the advertising literature put out by the development are usually the most attractive as well as the most expensive.

6 ARE YOU REALLY READY FOR ISLAND LIVING?

For some, the ideal if not the only place for a leisure home is on an island, and the more remote and private the island, the better. Happily for this group, there are a lot of islands around. There are, for example, around a thousand islands just along the coast of Maine, and heaven knows how many more scattered in our lakes, rivers, bays, gulfs, and seas. Islands come in all sizes and shapes.

By our definition, an island is a body of land completely surrounded by water that can only be reached from the mainland by boat or plane. If it is connected to the mainland by a bridge, in our book it's no island because the bridge eliminates all the interesting aspects of island living and building. A true island is something else again, and if living on an island, maybe even your own private island, is what you dream about, there are a few things you should know before you buy or build.

First is the fact that you may not be able to come and go as you please. Even a large modern ferry won't budge during a heavy storm, and fog will stop scheduled as well as private planes. Being on an island that is cut off from the mainland for a day or so can be very appealing at times, but it can also be a nuisance if you have to leave the island or get back to it. Even having to cross a lake in a bad storm in a small outboard can be an unpleasant and sometimes even dangerous experience.

Every leisure community or summer colony is bound to be a little clannish and informal, but island people seem to be especially so. Perhaps living on an island makes them that way, or perhaps islands attract people who are clannish and informal to start with. In any event, that is the way they are. If your idea of a vacation or summer weekend is to get away from people, you may have trouble doing it on an island, unless it is your own private island. It is always a good idea to see what kind of neighbors you are going to have before you settle in any vacation community, but it is particularly important in island living. You are going to be stuck with your neighbors for a good part of the time.

Islands are expensive to build on. No matter what sort of an island you choose, building on an island costs more than if you built the same house on the mainland. Your labor may not be any higher, but materials always will. Regardless of the size of the ferry or boats that serve the island, or how many trips they make, every item that goes into the house has to come across on them, and there will be a charge for every board and every nail. What's more, the materials have to be trucked to the dock on the mainland, unloaded, loaded onto the ferry, unloaded at the end of the voyage, loaded onto a truck, and hauled to the building site. This amount of handling can add a lot to your costs. Labor costs vary according to the type of island where you are building, but materials always cost more.

The best way to reduce your building costs on any island is to go with precut, panelized, or manufactured houses where large sections can be brought over instead of individual boards. If you insist on a stick-built house or are remodeling, eliminate as many nonessential items, such as trim, as you can. Each item you can eliminate without harming the design or efficiency of the house will save you money.

TYPES OF ISLANDS

Roughly speaking, there are three types of islands. Which one you decide to build on is going to influence what you build and how much it will cost.

Class A islands. These are the large islands with one or more settled communities and a rather high percentage of year-round residents. A local labor force will be available. There will also be several well-stocked building-supply houses, and although materials will cost somewhat more than on the mainland, at least most essential items will be on hand. Local outfits can drill a well if it is required, install a septic system, and so forth. On this type of island your building costs may run about 10 percent higher than on the mainland. It is the easiest type of island to build on and to live on. There will be plenty of shops open the year round, a doctor or two and a dentist. Living expenses will be higher than on the mainland and you won't be able to get the variety of goods you might want but you certainly won't be roughing it. And there will be a pretty fair mixture of people, so you'll have a lot of leeway in selecting friends.

Class B islands. These are something else again. As there is only a small year-round population there probably won't be too many workmen about, and they will be in heavy demand. It is not uncommon for families building vacation houses on this type of island to bring in workmen from the mainland and put them up in hotels or motels during the off season to build the house. What this does to building costs is to raise them considerably. There probably won't be much in the way of materials on the island, so that every item you require for your project will have to be ordered from the mainland. If you need a well, drilling equipment may have to be brought over from the mainland. There is no way to make a general statement on what your building costs will run, but before you decide to build, check with a local real estate broker, or a contractor on the island or on the mainland, and find out what building costs run per square foot.

Life on this type of island is going to be considerably more primitive than on the class A island. There will be fewer facilities, and many of them will only be open during the vacation season. There won't be a great variety of goods, and you'll be rather dependent on the mainland for anything out of the ordinary. You will find that the population is rather sharply divided between "summer people" and the natives, and as you are not a native you'll have to make friends among the vacation folk.

Class C islands. These are the kind to buy if you really want to get far away from people. They are private islands owned by one or a few families. Here there is nothing but a small amount of land surrounded by water and privacy. But don't forget that people with boats usually like to stop at islands to picnic or explore, so if you're going to own a whole or part of an island, be prepared for frequent unexpected visitors.

This is the most expensive as well as the most difficult type of island to build on. And once the house is finished, living on your island has a few problems.

Before you even begin to consider buying an island or part of one, find out what you can do about a water supply. If it's an island on a freshwater lake or river, and the water is relatively pure, you can use it for washing and bathing and bring in fresh water for drinking. But if it's an island on salt water, you've got to have a well, and if you need a deep well, you've got to have the means of getting the equipment across to the island and to the site. This means a pretty substantial wharf or deck.

You will, of course, need some sort of a dock in any event, and this is the first thing to build. You'll need it before you can even begin your house. You are also going to need a boat, and you should have one large enough so you'll be able to get back and forth in bad weather.

Build as simple a house as you can be comfortable in and equip it with stuff you can maintain yourself. If you can't, you had better learn how because it's not going to be easy to get a plumber or some other serviceman to come over each time you are having difficulty. What's more, when they do come, the charge will rock you off your feet.

Make up a complete set of all materials required for the house so they can be delivered in one shipment. You'll probably have to hire a large boat for this purpose, and if you can keep it down to one trip you'll save a lot of money. Also, a remote island is no place to run out of essential materials—it's a long haul to the nearest lumber yard or building-supply house.

How much it will cost you to build a vacation house on a class C island depends to a considerable degree on how far the island is from the mainland, the kind of transportation available (you can't carry many building supplies in a small outboard motor boat), and whether or not there is any electricity to run power tools, but it can run twice as much or more as building on the mainland. That's one reason we suggest keeping the house as simple as possible. The other reason is that you aren't going to be able to get fire insurance, and if the house ever does catch on fire, it will burn to the ground unless you can put out the fire yourself.

7

THE MINIMUM VACATION HOUSE

When we say "minimum" we mean it. We aren't talking about a house that is going to cost only a few thousand dollars—we are talking about one that is going to cost only a few hundred dollars. And it's going to be on the primitive side. It won't have plumbing, electricity, or any of the other modern conveniences. It will be the kind of place you build yourself out of the least expensive materials. But it will be a vacation house, and for the right kind of people it can be ideal, for it can offer a complete change from ordinary living and a sense of freedom that one finds only by getting down to essentials.

First, even for the most primitive house, you will need a piece of land. Not much land, but some, and you can either buy or rent it. If you can pick up some undeveloped land that appeals to you and that you can get for a song—fine. If not, consider renting a piece of ground. Renting rather than owning the land on which your house is built sort of goes against the American grain. Our heritage tells us that a man should own the land on which he builds his house. But there are parts of the country—Maryland and Hawaii, for example—where it has been common practice for years to rent land rather than own it outright. And for a primitive vacation house, renting makes sense. You don't have to raise a lot of cash to get the land; you can probably get a more attractive site than if you were buying on a limited budget; and you don't have any property tax to pay. Most important, renting the land will help you keep your place primitive—you won't want to invest too much in a structure you don't actually own. Unless you make arrangements with the owner of the land to remove anything you build, the structure will belong to him after your lease is up. The beauty of a primitive vacation house, of course, is that it makes a minimum number of demands on you and leaves you free to act, dress, and live exactly as you please.

RENTING LAND

You can often rent land from a private owner. Quite a few land-poor property owners—farmers and ranchers, for example—will jump at the opportunity to make a few dollars a year off a piece of land that isn't doing them any good. If their acreage is extensive, they may also like the idea of having someone around a remote section of it to keep an eye on things. You can often get leads to such private owners from real estate brokers or simply by asking around.

Certain companies such as paper, lumber, and mining outfits, who normally have large land holdings, also may have tracts for rent. Find out the names of companies that own land in the areas you are interested in and write to them, or write to the Recreation and Development Commission of the state and see if they can give you leads. Some state and federally owned land is also available for renting, and you can find out about it by writing to the appropriate state agency or to the U.S. Department of the Interior.

If you rent land you'll need some form of lease that states the amount of rent to be paid, the amount of land involved, and a right to access if getting to the land you are renting means crossing property not included in your parcel.

THE SITE

Regardless of whether you buy or rent, there are minimum requirements for the site. Naturally, it should be a pleasant place for a camp. There should be some sort of road leading into it. Although it's quite possible to live in an existing cabin or camp that can be reached only by trail or path, it's a darn nuisance to try to build when you have to lug every board and nail on foot. The longer the trail, the more nuisance it is.

There should also be some source of water within a reasonable distance. You can bring in enough bottled water for drinking and cooking, but hauling water for washing and bathing makes life hard. Water is a very heavy liquid: five gallons of water weigh close to forty pounds—more than five gallons of gasoline.

With a lake, pond, or healthy-looking stream or brook nearby, your water problem is solved. And the closer at hand it is, the better. If there is no obvious source of water, look for a spring or spot where you might dig a shallow well. You can usually locate a place where water is close to the surface without too much difficulty. In summer, look for any areas where the vegetation is especially green and lush. If the soil in these areas is more moist than the surrounding soil, it usually means water is not too far below the surface. In wet weather you may even find accumulations of water directly above a source. When the ground is covered by snow, look for spots where the snow has melted or has become thin or has a patch of ice on it. These are all indications of water below, close enough to the surface to have thawed the snow. When you believe you have found a place where there may be water, start digging—and hoping.

MINIMUM
HOUSES

The Primitive
Vacation House
Maine Coast

Photo 1. This one-room vacation house on the Maine coast was designed to serve as a shelter and storage place for camp living. It measures 12 by 8 feet and costs a total of $598.90. Walls are composition board with screened window spaces and plywood shutters hinged at the top. Four of the shutters open out to provide protection against rain. The floor is heavy plywood and the ceiling tongue-and-groove boards covered with roll roofing. The building is set on piers of stone. A carpenter built the shelter in sections in his workshop at a cost of $285.90 for materials and $128 for labor. He charged $8 to transport the prefabricated sections the 15 miles from his workshop, and an additional $177 for labor, which included paying helpers to carry the sections some 500 feet through the woods to the secluded campsite, where they put the structure together in a few hours.

Photo 2. Storage units in the shelter are all recycled containers and include vegetable crates (standing upright at left) for shelves; a Dutch tulip bulb box (hanging from wall in center) for dry food storage; and a metal potato chip cannister for mouseproof storage.

Photo 3. Two sleeping bags, easily stowed during the day, fit lengthwise; if placed crosswise, there is room for three or even four people.

Photo 4. Shelves are important to keep clutter under control, but otherwise furniture is superfluous.

Photo 5. The front door opens outward to save interior space.

Photo 6. Outdoor kitchen furniture is made entirely of driftwood. The "utilities" are a gasoline camp stove and a portable ice chest. Located under evergreen trees, the kitchen doesn't get much rain. But in a heavy downpour tarpaulins can be strung up overhead.

Photo 7. Instead of an enclosed privy, an earth closet was dug in a hillside sloping away from the camp and screened by a pile of brush. A tree and rock outcrop were used to support driftwood sit-upon and removable cover. Unslaked lime is used to hasten decomposition. A simple privy such as this can be relocated periodically if there is enough land and no danger of polluting water supply or swimming and fishing areas.

Photographs: Miller/Swift.

1

2

3

4

5

6

7

THE HOUSE

The easiest and quickest way to get a primitive vacation place is to pitch a tent. For around $150 you can pick up a good tent that can accommodate five people in a pinch and be quite comfortable for two. You will be more comfortable if you go to the extra effort and expense of putting the tent on a wood platform that will get you off the damp ground and will also provide a smooth floor. Tenting on the damp ground is not all that great, especially when the ground is wet rather than just damp. Also, although a dirt floor requires little maintenance, it's hard to get into bed at night without bringing some of the dirt in with you.

Tents now come with sewn-in vinyl-coated nylon floors, zippered mosquito-netted doors and windows, rain flaps, awnings, and other amenities the old-time camper never dreamed of. These features add to the expense, but if you are spending your vacation in a tent, you surely deserve some luxury—relatively speaking.

Most people who camp in the literal sense of pitching a tent also set up a permanent cooking and eating area that can be protected from rain when necessary. In fact, half the fun of this kind of vacation living seems to come from devising ingenious ways to solve problems that wouldn't even exist in a house. One problem, especially if you plan to use your camp only on weekends or for brief intervals whenever you can get there, is where to store your gear. This usually leads to putting up a permanent, lockable shelter either as a supplement to the tent or its replacement. A prefabricated metal shed of the kind sold by mail-order houses and lumber yards can be big enough—about 5 feet square—for storage alone. But if you want something with windows that you can sleep in, or where you can eat or read or play pinochle when it rains, you can build it or have it built for a few hundred dollars.

The first thing that may come to mind if you have a wooded lot is to build something out of logs. This is not such a hot idea. First, it takes a hell of a lot of logs to build even a modest-size house. And by modest we mean something around 8 feet by 12 feet. What's more, it takes a certain kind of log. Hardwood logs aren't much good because they're too uneven. Evergreens such as pine, balsam, and fir are all right if you can find enough of them with the same diameter and the right amount of taper, but that isn't always easy. Of course, you have to cut them down, trim off the branches, and notch them out accurately. Decaying somewhere in the northern Adirondacks is what remains of a log cabin we started to build years ago. Two of us worked on the place for the best part of a summer, and by the time our vacation was over, we had finally got the four walls almost finished. Unless you are in no hurry to complete your house, like a lot of hard work, and have plenty of the right type and size of trees, we'd suggest you forget about a handmade log cabin.

The minimum vacation house shown on page 58 is built out of conventional materials. It won't pass many building codes but it is solid and should stand up for a good many years.

Don't try to make a minimum house too big. In a 12-by-8 foot space you can fit four sleeping bags and if you make it 12-by-10 you can have two comfortable bunks with enough space left over for an overnight guest—if he or she brings a sleeping bag. Put the kitchen outdoors. It will not only save space but also eliminate a potential fire hazard. If you don't like cooking in the rain, put up a canvas tarp or build a shed over the cooking area. The bathroom, such as it is, should also be outside the house.

You don't have to worry much about foundations on a minimum house. Use flat rocks at the corners to support it. Build a platform out of 2 by 6's to serve as the floor. Cover with ¾-inch plywood or tongue-and-groove boards. Frame the roof out of 2 by 6's and cover with plywood or boards and use inexpensive roll roofing to make it watertight.

Frame the walls with 2 by 4's set 24 inches on center. Before you frame the walls, pick up your windows and doors. You may be able to get some secondhand at a salvage yard for practically nothing. All you need is the window sash—not the complete unit consisting of frame and sash. If you have your windows and doors on hand before you frame the walls, you can adjust the studding so that it forms the frame for sash and door. You'll need hinges to hang the door but the windows can be held in place with hooks or wing fasteners.

The outside walls can be covered with inexpensive exterior composition sheathing, exterior plywood, hardboard or asbestos board.

One vital point about building a minimum vacation house is to regard it as such and nothing more. If your plan is to start small and then add, don't build to minimum standards. Build to minimum size but use conventional building techniques— good foundations, proper framing, workable windows and so forth. For if you try to improve a minimum house, you'll find that you'll usually end up by pulling it down and starting off fresh.

8

HOW TO REDUCE BUILDING COSTS

The cost of building a vacation house—or any house for that matter —is determined by three primary factors: size, exterior design, and materials. If you want to keep your costs down, keep these points in mind when you build or buy.

SIZE

This is the most important element in determining the cost of a house. As a rule, the typical vacation house will run around $20 a square foot to build. It's pretty obvious, therefore, that the smaller the house, the less it will cost. You will be able to reduce your costs considerably if you select a plan or modify a plan so that it provides space for all your essential requirements but no more space than you really need—or can afford. A bedroom used primarily as a catchall, a living room far larger than you need, a dining room or dining area used only a couple of times each season, or an attached garage that merely stores miscellaneous junk are all expensive luxuries. For example, the average garage costs around $2,000 to build. Don't pay for space unless you need it—and need it all the time.

The less space you have, the more important it is to use what you have efficiently. As a matter of fact, it is possible to reduce the size of a house considerably and make it very comfortable if it is carefully planned so that the existing space is used well. And by efficient use of space we don't mean a house that is designed like a submarine or spaceship. Anyone with a pencil and ruler can draw up a floor plan of a small house, but it takes a talented and experienced architect to draw a plan that provides the greatest amount of comfortable living and storage space in the smallest area.

Good design means no wasted space. You find wasted space in halls, foyers, and landings. If their only purpose is to provide access to the various areas of the house, the plan is a poor one. A hall 3 feet wide by 10 feet long costs around $600. Poor planning often requires a room to be larger than is actually needed. If there are a lot of doors in a room, they reduce the amount of usable floor space. So, for that matter, do large expanses of glass running from floor to ceiling. As the space in front of the glass is no good for furniture, the room often has to be larger just to get a place to put things.

The size of many rooms can be reduced without impairing their function. Bedrooms in a vacation house, especially those to be used by children or guests, don't have to be spacious—the kids should be outdoors and the guests shouldn't be made so comfortable that they'll never go home. If bunk beds are used, one bedroom can accommodate two people in the same amount of space a single bed requires.

Built-in furniture is a great space saver, but unless it is kept simple it costs so much it eliminates any saving. Space in a house can also be saved by making one area serve several purposes. A good example is the open kitchen at one end of the living room. With such an arrangement, the living room serves three functions—kitchen, dining room, and living area. If you need extra sleeping accommodations from time to time, a built-in sofa or sofa bed in the living room helps too.

Good planning also saves money in the construction of a house. If kitchen and bathrooms are grouped in the same general area, for example, it can make a considerable difference in plumbing cost. And a compact house costs less to heat in winter and to cool in summer than a rambling one.

EXTERIOR DESIGN

The basic design of the house will have considerable effect on its cost. It costs less to build a square house than a rectangular one of equal size. It costs less to build a rectangular house than an L-shaped one. It costs less to build a two-story or story-and-a-half house than a one-story house with the same amount of space. Where soil conditions are right —easy to excavate and no subsurface water—below-grade construction can often be less expensive than above-grade, which makes the split-level house a good buy for the money.

The least expensive houses are those with a rather simple design that can be built with conventional materials and with conventional methods of construction. We are speaking now only of stick-built houses. When you get into manufactured houses—precut, prefab, and modular—it's the unconventional method of construction that saves you money.

MATERIALS

What the house is built from is going to have a lot to do with what it costs. You can add thousands of dollars to the cost of a house simply by selecting the more expensive building materials. We asked an architect who specializes in vacation houses what the average cost was per square foot. He said there was no average because the cost was completely dependent on what the client selected in the way of materials. Some houses this architect designed came in at $20 a square foot and some came in at $35. It was all a question of materials.

Remember, it's not just the original cost of the materials to consider—it's what they cost after you have paid for the labor to install them. Roughly half the total cost of a house goes for labor. This can produce some strange situations. For example, you may have a site with a lot of native stone sitting around just waiting to be used for the fireplace and chimney and even the outside walls of the house. You can have the stone for nothing, but by the time you've paid for the labor to put it up, you would have been far better off financially to have used brick, which you would have had to buy. It takes a lot more labor to lay a square yard of uncut native stone than it does to lay the same amount of brick.

Before you select materials for your house, therefore, go over the "cost installed" with your architect, contractor, or whoever it is who is doing the work. And keep asking what other, less expensive materials are available than the ones they suggest. Everybody in the building business, even architects, gets hung up on certain materials and likes to use them on every job. We know one architect who loves cedar shingles for vacation houses and will use them anyplace he can find a spot for them. We also know a plumbing contractor whose arm almost has to be twisted off before he'll admit that colored plumbing fixtures, which he likes, cost more than white ones. So keep bugging them on costs.

Here are a few examples of how different materials for a house compare in cost installed.

Masonry. The least expensive type installed is concrete block. Poured concrete can be less expensive on a large job, but as a rule, concrete block is your best bet for foundations. It can also be used for a chimney and even for a fireplace, if the interior is lined with firebrick. After block, brick is the least expensive, and then stone.

In the warmer sections of the country—Florida and the

Southwest—building the outside walls of a house out of masonry block is a common practice and is a method of construction both practical and inexpensive. Not so in colder areas. To prevent condensation and sweating in cold weather, the interior side of the walls must be covered with another wall surface.

Framing lumber. Here you take what is locally available. It is usually Douglas fir or hemlock. You can save some money on the cost of framing lumber by using 2-by-3-inch stock rather than 2-by-4-inch material wherever possible.

Many vacation houses are designed so that some framing elements such as roof rafters are left exposed. This is economical if the wood is left rough and stained but if the framing material is to be given a smooth finished appearance, either expensive framing materials must be used or a lot of money spent on the labor to smooth and finish the rough stuff.

Siding. You'll find a wide variation in prices here so check this one out carefully with your contractor or carpenter. Generally speaking, the least expensive siding is plywood. Reverse board and batten plywood siding is attractive and available just about anyplace. It can be finished with a pigmented exterior stain which is good because a stain is less expensive than paint. Cedar shingles come next followed by cedar clapboard, aluminum, and vinyl siding. Redwood makes an excellent and very durable siding but it's expensive in most sections of the country.

In certain areas, such as the Southeast, Northeast, and Northwest, you may find local lumber mills where you can get wood siding and other wood products at less than you would pay through a local lumber yard. If there are some around, be sure to check them out.

Roofing. Asphalt shingles are the least expensive roofing material suitable for a house. They can be used on almost every kind of roof except those that are almost flat. On these you must use a built-up roof. For a minimum-cost vacation house, roll roofing is adequate and costs even less than asphalt shingles, but because of its appearance it is not recommended for anything except minimum construction. Wood shingles are considerably more expensive than asphalt shingles.

Windows. There are two types of windows: double hung, where there are two window sashes that move up and down, and casement, where the sash is hinged to the frame like a door. The double-hung unit is the less expensive of the two.

The two most commonly used materials for window frames are aluminum and wood. Aluminum is less expensive. Aluminum windows with a natural finish cost even less and are satisfactory except near salt water where excessive oxidation can be a problem. If the house is near the ocean, use aluminum windows with a baked enamel or bronze finish. An even more expensive type of aluminum window comes with a coating of plastic which the manufacturer claims eliminates a major drawback to aluminum windows—a tendency of the frame on the inside to sweat in very cold weather.

Good-quality wood window frames cost more than aluminum ones, but they often look better, especially in more traditionally designed houses. The least expensive ones come unfinished but the wood is treated with a wood preservative. The best ones come with a coating of plastic over the wood which eliminates the need for painting.

Windows come in stock sizes, and a wide variety of sizes and styles is available. If your plans call for special-size units, they will have to be custom made, which is rather expensive. Better to change your plans and use stock sizes.

Screens and storm windows. In practically every section of the country, window screens are necessary to keep flies and bugs out of the house. If the house is going to be used in cold weather, you will need either storm windows or windows made from insulating glass. Therefore, the best type of windows to buy are the kind that come with screens and storm sash. These units, purchased separately, cost around $20 per window, installed.

Sliding glass doors. These are made of aluminum or wood, and the aluminum ones are less expensive. The better-quality units of both types come with safety glass which is worth the extra money it costs. If you are going to use the house in winter, specify doors made of insulating glass. They are expensive but will save unnecessary heat loss and make the house more comfortable in cold weather.

In new construction a sliding glass door may not cost any more than it would to cover the same area with a solid wall. But when it comes to remodeling, the cost of installing the unit may be rather high because of the need for additional support around the door opening.

Doors. If you have a carpenter who works at a reasonable rate, he can probably make up a batten type of door that will cost less than a factory-built unit. This type of door, however, is suitable only in rustic or rather casual vacation houses. As far as factory units go, the hollow-core door is the least expensive and is good for interior work except for bathrooms and any other areas where you may want a more soundproof door. For these locations, and for exterior doors, use solid-core doors or a heavy panel door.

Sliding doors made of particle board are also good for closets; they are not only inexpensive but don't take up valuable floor space the way a hinged door does. You can save a little money in framing and make the upper part of a closet more accessible if you run closet doors from floor to ceiling.

Flooring. Stay away from stone, tile, slate, and other forms of masonry if you have a budget problem. Vinyl asbestos is the least expensive flooring, followed by linoleum and vinyl. In some situations wood can be a good buy, so get your contractor or carpenter to give you a price comparison between wood and the other flooring materials.

Interior wall surfaces. If your vacation house is to be a summer house only, the least expensive way to treat the inside walls is not to cover them at all but to leave the framing and siding exposed. These surfaces can be painted or stained if you wish or permitted to darken naturally. The best buy in wall surfacing is gypsum board. It can be used in every room of the house—even in the bath and kitchen. When you add the cost of painting or papering it, the price per square foot will still be less than anything else you can use.

Plywood paneling is also relatively inexpensive and so are some of the wall products made of hardboard. The cost of individual board paneling is relatively high. The least expensive will be locally cut boards and the most expensive will be redwood.

Plumbing. If local codes permit, use plastic pipe for your drainage system. It costs considerably less than copper, galvanized iron, or cast iron, and it can be installed with a lot less labor. Also, if you are going to have your own water system, use plastic pipe rather than copper from the water supply to the pump. Copper is an excellent material but it is expensive. Plastic pipe can also be used in place of copper for the cold-water lines inside the house—if codes permit. Certain types are also suitable for hot-water lines.

You can save several hundred dollars on a house in plumbing fixtures alone. To install a fixture costs the same whatever its style or color, but there can be a big difference in cost between different models. Colored fixtures, for example, are considerably more expensive than white ones. There can be a difference of a hundred dollars or more just between two lavatories, or between two kinds of toilets or bathtubs. And there is a big difference in price between standard fittings—faucets, drains, etc., and deluxe ones. The price variations do not occur so much from one manufacturer to another—except on some of the off-brand and mail-order stuff, which is considerably less than the nationally advertised fixtures—as between the relatively simple as compared to fancy designs.

A fiberglass shower stall is less expensive than a bathtub.

If you are considering built-in lavatories, the final cost will include the cabinet work required as well as the fixture itself. You may find that when you add these costs together, you are not getting any bargain and would be better off to use the free-standing units that don't require custom-made cabinets.

The kitchen. If you don't watch yourself, a kitchen can become an expensive proposition. Deluxe models of anything cost more than bottom-of-the-line appliances without fancy gadgets and gimmicks, so you will save a good deal of money on a range, dishwasher, and refrigerator if you keep them simple.

Cabinets and counters are costly items in kitchens. The ready-made ones are expensive but the fancy, custom-made ones are even more so. About the best way to reduce costs here is to have a carpenter build the simplest type of unit out of inexpensive materials such as plywood or particle board. Linoleum is a far less expensive covering for countertops than laminated plastic and simple sliding doors cost less than hinged ones. And whatever you do, resist the urge to have more cabinets and counters than you really need.

Fireplace. A metal, prefabricated fireplace costs about half as much as one made of brick, and a brick fireplace costs less than one of stone. In either case, you'll save money if you don't have the masonry exposed all the way up to the ceiling. If the masonry above the mantel is covered by gypsum board, it doesn't have to be finished with the same care.

Paints and finishes. The least expensive finish for exterior wood siding is no finish at all—just let the wood weather. The only disadvantage to this is that those areas that get the most exposure will weather more rapidly than the protected sections. This problem can be eliminated by coating the wood with a pigmented wood sealer or stain. This is less expensive than paint.

For interior walls other than wood, paint is the least expensive coating, followed by wallpaper and then vinyl fabric. For interior woodwork, a clear or pigmented wood sealer is less expensive than paint.

DO IT
YOURSELF

About half the cost of building a vacation house goes into labor; the other half goes into materials. If you want to save a lot of money, build the house yourself. Before you decide to go this route, however, and especially if you decide to build the house from scratch, you should have some idea of what you are letting yourself in for.

It takes an awfully long time to build a house—even a modest house—if you are doing it alone on weekends and during your two- or three-week vacation. It is not unusual for such a project to drag on for years.

Building a house is hard physical work. You may have the will to work twelve hours a day, but unless you have the physical stamina, your effective work day may dwindle to four or five hours. And you will need a little ordinary brute strength to handle roof rafters, lift window units into place, and haul concrete blocks. Remember, too, that a certain amount of physical risk is involved in any kind of heavy construction. If you aren't in good physical shape, or aren't careful, you may end up with pulled muscles, a sprained back, a hernia, or a broken arm or leg.

If these cautions don't deter you, some local building codes may. In most organized communities some form of building code is in effect and it usually specifies that certain work, such as electric wiring and plumbing, be done by licensed mechanics. There may also be a tough building inspector who will visit the job frequently and who has the authority to make you redo any work he feels is not structurally sound. Still, there are fewer building codes in the back country, and often no one is around to enforce the few that are on the books. And plenty of families have built their own houses—vacation or otherwise—from scratch.

For the do-it-yourselfer we highly recommend buying a precut shell house or remodeling an existing house. The precut shells are a whale of a lot easier to put up than a stick-built house, and with an existing house you already have a completed shell. But if you decide to work from the ground up, here are some words of advice.

Start out small. It is better to build a small house that you'll be able to finish in a reasonable length of time (and perhaps add on to later) than to attempt a large project that you'll be working on for years.

Select a simple design. A square or rectangular house is your best bet. Anything with wings or extensions is complicated to build. Use a design with a shed or pitched roof. Keep clear of anything with two or more different roof pitches because they are very hard to frame and to cover with shingles.

Don't build a two-story house. Two stories may give you the most house for the money, but they are more complicated to build than a one-story house. You'll need to carry a lot of materials to the upper level and roof, and you'll require a lot of special scaffolding. You can also hurt yourself a lot worse falling off a two-story house than a one-story job.

Use simple and inexpensive materials. Wood is the best bet for the do-it-yourselfer, so use it wherever you can. With a little practice almost anyone can learn to measure and cut a board to the right length and nail it in place, but laying bricks or even concrete blocks properly is something that looks a lot easier than it really is.

Get all the information and help you can. If you have never built a house before or had much experience in building anything, you've got a lot to learn before you start work. Fortunately, several good sources can supply this kind of help.

You can learn a lot by reading. A number of books on house construction are designed for the amateur as well as the professional. You can find them at larger bookstores and at your local library. You won't learn everything you need to know by reading one book, but if you read several you'll be off to a good start as an amateur builder. The federal government has published a lot of good information on all aspects of home construction. Some of the material is pretty dated, but it still applies in many instances. You can get a catalogue of government literature on homes by writing to the Superintendent of Documents, Washington, D.C. 20402, and asking for *price list 72.*

Also try writing various associations. The Portland Cement Association, 510 North Dearborn Street, Chicago, Illinois 60610, has a lot of very good material on the use of concrete and cement products. The National Forest Products Association, 1619 Massachusetts Avenue, N.W., Washington, D.C. 20036; Ponderosa Pine Woodwork, 39 S. LaSalle Street, Chicago, Illinois 60603; Red Cedar & Shake Association, Seattle, Washington 98100; and Western Wood Products, Portland, Oregon 97200 can furnish you with material on the use of various wood products. About the best book on the subject of electric wiring is put out by Sears, Roebuck. Even if you don't plan to do the wiring yourself, it's very helpful in planning what you require.

While you can learn a good deal by reading, you won't find everything you need to know in print. A local lumber yard or building-supply house can help you solve special problems or answer particular questions. The same holds true of a good hardware store. You'll probably get more personalized service if you establish credit, let them know you are building a house, and don't come around early in the morning when they are busy dealing with contractors. And many lumber yards will give you a discount if you buy all your materials from them.

As you get into the back country, it is easier to do things yourself because a lot of other people there are doing the same thing. In rural areas homeowners do a lot more than simple paint and carpentry jobs. They do masonry work, install plumbing, heating, wiring, and practically anything else that is needed. A lot of business concerns in country areas cater to this market. In the country you will find building-supply houses that sell everything—lumber, masonry items, plumbing fixtures and pipe, electric wiring, windows, all kinds of floor, roofing, and so on. And a good many will be very helpful.

We once remodeled a summer cottage in a rather chic little community and had a terrible time because none of the local stores had anything we needed. The hardware store had plenty of summer outdoor furniture and marine equipment but none of the heavy construction hardware we required, and the local lumber yard wasn't even open on Saturdays. Then we moved out into a do-it-yourself area where the hardware store cut and threaded pipe to order and some of the lumber yards stayed open until eight o'clock Saturday nights.

A great boon to the do-it-yourselfer is being able to rent specialized tools. You'll find tool rental outfits all over, and they carry everything under the sun, from a portable 1/4-inch electric drill to a gasoline-powered trench digger. You can rent power chain saws, table saws, scaffolding, earth-moving equipment, plumbing tools, and practically anything else you might need. Being able to rent tools at a nominal cost is a great help; equally important, the clerk will be able to tell you how to use the equipment.

Today's new materials also make it easier to do your own

work. We aren't talking about basic materials, because you can't beat wood for our money, but about some of the other elements that go into the house. Take plastic pipe, for example. This stuff is almost as easy to work with as it is to connect lengths of garden hose. It can be used for hot-water lines, and it's ideal for cold-water lines and for the drainage system. Metal framing anchors are another great invention. These are metal plates in different shapes that are used to fasten together two pieces of framing. They not only ensure a solid joint but eliminate the need to make difficult angle cuts and notches in roof rafters and other structural members. They come with predrilled holes for nails which eliminates the great problem faced by most amateur builders—how many nails to use to make the joint solid. Plastic-covered electrical wiring is far easier to work with than the old BX cable with its metal covering, and it is approved by most electrical codes. Spend a few hours looking around a good lumber yard, building-supply house, and hardware store and you'll run into a lot of practical new items.

TOOLS YOU NEED

You don't need an awful lot of tools to frame a house. Basically you need a good claw hammer, a crosscut saw, a steel rule, framing square, level, and that's about it. It will speed up the job considerably if you buy or rent a portable 7 1/2-inch electric saw. When you get into the interior work, more specialized tools—chisels, planes, screwdrivers, keyhole saws—will be required. Buy good-quality hand tools. They do a better job and last longer than the inexpensive ones. On items such as crowbars, sledgehammers, picks, and even shovels that you may need for foundations and trenches, get secondhand ones if you can. They do the job as well as the new ones and they cost a lot less.

HOW TO GET STARTED

You need plans to build a house yourself—as much if not more than if you hire a carpenter or contractor. You need the plans not only as a guide but also to determine exactly how each step must be done to make it ready for the next step. Items such as doors and windows, for example, come in stock sizes, and the rough opening made in the walls must be made to the exact dimensions to accommodate a certain type of unit. If you haven't planned the job and don't know what size windows or doors you are going to use, you can't make the correct-size openings. Draw up your plans and then get window and door catalogues from your lumber dealer so that you can determine the proper size for the rough openings.

There is a sequence to building a house and you should follow it. And don't move to the next step until the previous step is complete—and is done right. For if you don't get it right you'll end up with a lot of problems, some of which can't be corrected later.

The foundations are the first things to go in. They must be level and true; if they are not, your house isn't going to be level and true. A fine carpenter once told us he turned down the chance to build a very expensive house because the man who was going to put in the foundations did poor work and the carpenter knew he'd have a great deal of difficulty putting up a good house on a poor foundation. It will usually pay in the long run to get a good professional to put in the foundations unless you have enough experience in this area to do an excellent job.

Once the foundations are in, the next step is the framing. Take the time to make certain the walls are plumb because if they are not, you'll have a lot of trouble trying to get doors to swing properly. Once the walls and roof are framed, cover them with sheathing—walls first and then roof. Apply the roofing and then put in the windows and outside doors. Now the house is weathertight. When you can't work outdoors, you can work indoors.

Exterior siding can be applied and this about finishes work on the outside of the house. On the interior, frame the partitions first. After these are up, the rough wiring can be put in along with the rough plumbing and the bathtub. The bathtub has to come in early—it may not fit through a finished door!

The next step is to put in the interior door frames and then apply the wall and ceiling material. After these are in place, the finish electrical and plumbing work can be done along with installing such things as the kitchen cabinets. The final step is painting the interior and exterior.

BUY AND
REMODEL

In your search for a moderate-cost vacation house, by all means consider buying an existing structure and remodeling it. You probably already know some of the disadvantages of this approach: It takes a lot of time and effort, plus a lot of headaches, to fix up any kind of existing structure. It usually costs more money than you or anyone else figured. Chances are you won't end up with your ideal house. And there are probably more drawbacks. But consider the advantages: First and most important is that it may be the only way to get a desirable piece of property. This is especially true of recreational areas relatively near large population centers. These vacation communities were built up years ago, and today there isn't a vacant piece of land in the vicinity. (Or if there is, the owner is probably holding out for a price that can be justified only by putting a very expensive house on it.) But if there is a beat-up summer cottage, a run-down farmhouse, a garage, a barn, or some sort of structure already on the property, you can sometimes get both land and structure at a fairly reasonable price.

Another big plus to buying and remodeling is that, if the place is at all livable, you can start using it immediately. It's an ideal situation for the do-it-yourselfer, for you can live in and enjoy the place and work at it at your own pace. Finally, it is usually easier to get financing on property that includes some sort of a structure.

WHAT TO LOOK FOR

This depends on your budget and where you are looking. If you are flush and aren't looking in the most popular areas, you may find a house in pretty fair shape —even winterized. If you are not so affluent and looking in a high-cost community, keep an eye out for anything that has a structure on it—a large garage, barn, rundown roominghouse, or anything with walls and a roof. We've seen families who have made fine vacation houses out of sheep barns, nondescript farmhouses, old hotels, schoolhouses, and even World War II radar towers. But the most common type of structures available are the ticky-tacky little summer cottages in need of a lot of basic improvements and repairs. And in the right location, these can be made into good vacation houses.

The best way to look for a structure to remodel is to get a real estate broker. It doesn't cost you anything and can save you a lot of time and effort. Select a community you want to check out and then visit a local broker. Go to a broker who belongs to a multiple-listing association, for he will have a wider selection than a broker who does not handle listings from other brokers. It has been our experience that women brokers get the picture of what you are looking for faster than male brokers. Men seem more inclined to try and push property way beyond your means and it takes a bit of time before they finally get around to showing you stuff you can afford.

Explain what you are looking for and in what price range. The broker will then pull out a bunch of cards that show photographs and give pertinent information on dwellings in that category. If you see something you are interested in, he can take you to inspect the property. If nothing suits your needs, leave your name and address in case a new listing comes up, and move along to another area.

You don't have to use a broker, of course. You can find property advertised for sale in local newspapers. If you have friends living in the area, they may give you leads or even inside tips on property that will shortly be on sale. Driving around and looking for *For Sale* signs can also be effective. Many states and communities put out pamphlets with real estate listings. You can usually get these by writing to the chamber of commerce at the state capital or from the state recreational and development commission. By and large, however, a broker is your best bet.

ESTIMATING COSTS

When you find something of interest, there are many things you should check out before you get too involved and sign any papers or write any checks. First and foremost is the condition of the structure and what it will cost in time and money to make it into a pleasant vacation house. You can get a pretty fair idea of what sort of shape a building is in just by giving it a close inspection and questioning the seller or broker as to the condition of the roof, foundations, outside walls, plumbing, and wiring.

Here are some of the major costs you can incur in remodeling a structure.

1. Water supply: If you need a well, figure about $1,500 complete.

2. If the house needs a septic system, figure $350.

3. Inside plumbing including one bathroom and the kitchen sink costs about $1,000.

4. Electric wiring runs $450 or so.

6. Reroofing a modest-size structure with asphalt shingles, figure another $400 or more.

7. Repainting the outside of the house can run from $300 to $500.

The only way to get a true idea of what fixing up a structure will cost, however, is to get in an expert. In some communities engineers or architects will evaluate property and give you an estimate of what the remodeling will cost for a fee of $50, $100, or more. If you can't get hold of one of these men, call in a local builder or general contractor. He can give you a quick but rough estimate on what he feels will be involved, and this will be a much more accurate picture than what the seller or his broker may tell you. It's not that they are dishonest, but they simply can't know the field as well as an experienced contractor. You may have to pay the contractor something for his estimate, but if you buy the house and have him do the work, he'll probably credit you with the amount you paid him for his time and effort.

Once you get an estimate from a qualified individual on what it is going to cost to put the property into shape, you are in a position to evaluate the property realistically. You may be able to reduce the cost of basic improvements by eliminating some of them or by doing a portion of the work yourself. You may be able to find a contractor who will do the work for less than the one who made the original estimate. In any event, you'll have some solid figures to go by.

There are also some other important areas to explore early in the game and one of these is our old friend—sewage disposal. Unless the community where the dwelling is located is served by city sewer lines—rather unlikely—your structure will have a septic tank, a cesspool, or nothing. More and more communities are becoming concerned about sewage, especially where there are a lot of houses close together on small lots or near a body of water that sewage runoff can pollute. If the place you are looking at does not now have a sewage system—which might be true of a barn or garage—local regulations might prohibit your putting in a system. In that event, the place is out as far as a residence goes. Even if the structure does have a sewage system, regulations may prohibit your using the existing system. Some states and many communities now have laws saying that when a house is sold, the buyer must improve the sewage facilities to meet new requirements. For example, if you bought a house that had a workable cesspool, you still might have to put in an expensive septic system before you could get a permit to use the house as a residence. Some communities have regulations that prohibit your adding another bathroom or even winterizing the house so it can be used the year round. The theory here is the soil can absorb just so much liquid waste, and each bathroom means the addition of more waste. When houses are used for the summer only, the soil is better able to absorb the waste than if they are used year round and the soil has no chance to recover.

Local regulations may also govern what you can do with a place and how the work must be done. You may find, for example, that there is a regulation that forbids remodeling a large place to make it suitable for two families or for a rental apartment. Other regulations may require extensive changes in the house wiring or plumbing system.

What you had better do before you decide to make an offer on the property is to get down to the local city hall and talk with the local building inspector, the zoning board, and other housing officials. Explain to them exactly what you plan to do with the property and how you are going to use it and then see if they will allow it.

FINANCING

We discussed methods of financing in Chapter 4, but let us say again that the best way to finance the purchase of an existing house and the cost of fixing it up is with a mortgage loan that includes a construction loan. This package can provide certain of the money you will require to purchase and fix up the place. It is by far the best approach. You should be prepared to show the lender what you plan in the way of improvements and also the cost. And the cost should be based on an estimate from a local contractor and not a guess on your part or on the part of the broker or seller.

You should certainly have your lawyer examine the agreement for sale before you sign it and examine the title to the property not only to make sure that it is clear but also that you can use it as you so intend. Buying property with a structure on it is just as complicated as any other real estate transaction, and having an attorney to handle certain phases of the transaction is absolutely essential.

PLANNING THE REMODELING

Remodeling an existing structure can be much more involved than planning a new house. You have to work pretty much with what you have. Careful planning before you begin work is essential if you want to get good results and hold down costs. One of the reasons why many families have so much trouble remodeling is that they move ahead too fast, before they really know what they want, and do not carefully plan the project in advance.

If the structure needs extensive planning, it is worth the time and money to hire an architect. Even if you can't afford to commission an architect to handle a major portion of the work, it is worth spending $50 to $100 to have one come over, inspect the place, and draw up a rough plan of what he considers a good approach to the problem. A contractor can also be helpful in working with you on the plans for a remodeling, but he will seldom be as imaginative as an architect.

For those working on a limited budget who want to pay for the remodeling out of income over a period of years, it pays to plan the project so that it can be done in stages without making the house unlivable in the meantime. Some families, for example, have done the living room first so there would be one finished room for family and friends. They let the kitchen, baths, and bedrooms go until later on, then finish the kitchen first, then the baths, and finally the bedrooms.

11

THE ARCHITECT

Architects have been responsible for some very expensive and, in our opinion, some very horrible-looking vacation houses. They have also designed some of the best modest-cost vacation houses you can find.

A residential architect has a wealth of knowledge on just about everything connected with a house. He knows about house design, materials, construction, land and land development, landscaping, and even interior decorating. He can design a new house for you, plan a remodeling, or evaluate an existing house. He can help you select a piece of land, choose a builder, and pick the color of the paint for the living room walls. It's a darn shame there aren't more architects and that more people don't feel they can afford one, because if you have an architect on your side, you'll not only avoid mistakes and headaches, but he can even save you money.

An architect can save you money in several ways. First, by imaginative design he can fit all your requirements into less space, and this means considerable saving on construction costs. Second, he can make imaginative use of low-cost materials, and this, too, means a substantial saving. If you get to him early enough, he can even save you money on the purchase of land. Some years ago a family, vacation-house bent, were out looking over land with their architect and a broker. One of the parcels they saw was a small wooded lot with a nice low price and a beautiful view. It had only one flaw: a rocky ravine ran right through the middle of the lot, and there wasn't enough land on either side for a house. Later, over a drink, the architect sketched on a napkin what he would suggest for that site—a bridge house that spanned the ravine. The family liked the idea, bought the land for a song, and built the house. Needless to say, if you already own a problem site and you can't see how to build on it, get hold of an architect.

SELECTING AN ARCHITECT

There are a lot of architects about. Not all of them are great and not all of them are interested in low- or moderate-cost vacation houses. Your best bet is likely to be a young architect who has done a fair number of vacation houses in your price range and doesn't look upon your commission as an opportunity to make a philosophical "statement."

If you are building in an area with a lot of vacation-house activity, you may find your architect right there. A good many younger architects have their practice in these locations because, aside from having an attractive place to live and work, they find designing and building vacation houses more fun and more challenging than designing just another $75,000 Colonial-style house or a suburban supermarket.

One advantage in using an architect who works in the same area where you plan to build is that he is familiar with the local situation—the availability of materials, the quality of local workmanship, and any other special problems of that sort. This knowledge can be important to you as the client. We heard of one family whose architect, a big-city dweller, called for a flat roof on the house he designed. When it came time to

ARCHITECTURAL
HOUSES

The Architect-designed House
*Waterfront Beach House,
Branford, Connecticut*

A lot of living space is packed into an area approximately 18 by 25 feet in this contemporary house designed by architect Caswell Cooke of New Haven, Connecticut. Because of the small size of the waterfront lot overlooking Long Island Sound, Cooke decided to use a multilevel approach in order to achieve the feeling of openness and spaciousness that both he and his client wanted. There was a natural slope of the land toward the water on the south, so he was able to gain an extra half-level on the north side of the house, where a short flight of outside steps leads into entryway and onto a balcony. Stairs descend to the lower level of a high-ceilinged living room that is open to bedroom level above, as shown on the floor plan. With this arrangement it was possible to build extra storage space and a guest bunk bed into the balcony level, where another short flight of stairs leads to bedrooms above. This house was brought to completion for under $25,000 which included appliances, built-in furniture, and fixtures.

Photos 1 and 2. Strong vertical lines of glass on west wall add interest to the simple boxlike structure. Glass is double-glazed and tinted to keep out the hot western sun but still admit light. Entry steps on north wall are shown at right. North and east walls, the ones most exposed to winds and winter storms, are almost entirely siding. All siding is Douglas Fir plywood.

Photo 3. Generous use of glass on south (water) side permits view of Sound from every level while bathing interior in soft, south light.

Photo 4. Bold architectural detailing and soaring line of fireplace chimney combine dramatic visual impact with practical utilization of space. Kitchen, seen behind fireplace, is functional and compact without being cramped. It is open to a skylight above, which gives pleasant, even light to area.

Floor plan. Waterfront Beach House.

2

3

4

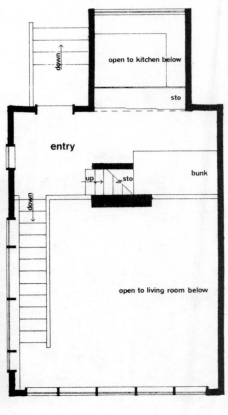

down

open to kitchen below

sto

entry

up → sto

bunk

down

open to living room below

entry-level plan

10 ft

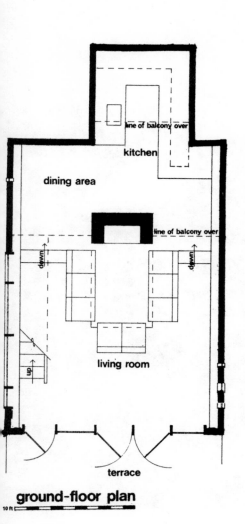

dining area

kitchen

line of balcony over

line of balcony over

down

down

up

living room

terrace

ground-floor plan

10 ft

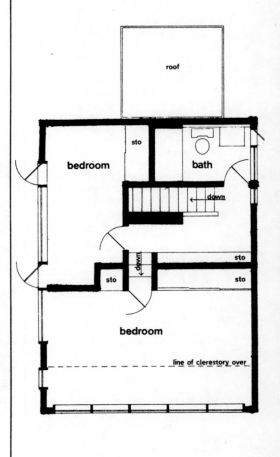

roof

sto

bedroom

bath

down

down

sto

sto

sto

bedroom

line of clerestory over

second-floor plan

10 ft

The Custom-built House

*Mountain house,
New Hampshire*

This handsome and unusual house-cum-boat house built on a lake in the New Hampshire mountains was designed by Randall Thompson, Jr., of Cambridge, Massachusetts. The client, who owns several thousand acres of the surrounding land, wanted the house primarily as a retreat where his children could bring their friends for weekends and summer vacations.

Photo 1. Built half on the lake and half on the shore, the house is a hexagon, 53 feet in diameter. Canoe racks, work benches, and clothes bins are built into the ground-floor level with stairs leading to the first floor which, with the exception of two bath-dressing rooms and a master bedroom is entirely open. Window walls and sliding glass doors open onto the hexagonal surrounding deck filling the house with light and views of the outdoors. The house is sheathed with mahogany clapboards; decking is of cypress; and the roof is Canadian cedar shingles. Obviously a house of this quality designed entirely to the wishes of the client is not within the reach of everyone. Exact-cost figures are not available but as J. P. Morgan said when asked how much it cost to run his yacht, "If you have to ask how much it costs—you can't afford it." That about sums it up.

Photo 2. Kitchen-dining area shows details of custom-designed-and-built cabinets, wall oven, and rafter-concealed lighting. Refrigerator and sink bar are on right.

Photo 3. Numerous built-in benches make comfortable beds when topped with guests' sleeping bags. Circular metal fireplace leading eventually into masonry chimney provides cheer and heat, since house is not used in cold weather.

Photo 4. Structural details are elegantly simple, as shown in this view of exterior and steps leading to lower level, open deck.

Photographs: William Maris.

1

4

put on the roofing, it turned out that no one in the area was qualified to do the job and a roofing outfit from about 65 miles away had to be called in. This raised the cost of the roof considerably.

Another advantage of having a local architect is that he can inspect the job frequently. He can go to the site personally when a problem arises rather than trying to solve it over the long-distance telephone or by letter. On the other hand, plenty of good houses have been designed and built by architects who were not on hand every minute. It depends on the house, the area where it is being built, the contractor, and the architect.

You can get the names of architects who specialize in vacation houses from a local real estate broker, local banks, building inspectors, and even lumber yards. You might also watch local newspapers as well as home and leisure magazines, for their work often appears in these publications. In a pinch you can call any architect and he will usually give you the names of other architects who do vacation houses.

There are two essential points in the selection of an architect: you should like the kind of work he has already done, and you should like him. This is especially true if you are going to have him design a house for you or do a remodeling where you will be working together for a while. If you need an architect merely to give you his opinion on a piece of land, the condition of an existing house, or to make minor changes in a stock floor plan, it probably doesn't make much difference if you like him or he likes you. But if he is going to do an entire house for you, it's important that you get along and that your tastes are more or less the same.

You can find out about an architect's work easily enough by asking him to show you what he has done. Look over some of his previous plans and pictures for vacation houses. If he has built some houses in the area, go with him and take a look at them. If you like what you see, discuss your project with him and see how he responds. If he shows enthusiasm and interest, and you feel you can get along, he may be your man.

HOW MUCH DOES AN ARCHITECT COST?

This depends on how much he is going to do for you. If he is going to handle the entire job, the usual method is to base the fee on a percentage of the total cost of construction. The standard fee is about 15 percent, but some architects charge more—maybe 20 percent. And this is also what most charge on a remodeling because of the amount of time required in relationship to the construction cost. If your architect's fee is 15 percent and you are building a house that will cost $20,000, his fee will be $3,000. That's a lot of money, but you'll get a lot for it. When the architect takes over the entire operation, he does just that. He'll listen to what you want in a house, make rough sketches, and when he finally has something you like, he'll do finished drawings and even renderings so you can see how the finished house will look.

If you don't own land, he'll help you select a good site for the house. He will help you select materials and products for the house and will usually tell you about items you never knew existed. He will write up the specifications detailing exactly how the work is to be done. He will help you select a contractor and will supervise the construction so that it is done in the manner both you and he want. When problems crop up, he will solve them for you. He will be the one who deals with the contractor and he'll make sure that you don't pay for anything you don't get, or anything that is not done in accordance with the specifications. As far as you are concerned, once you have approved the plans you can go off and not be back until the house is finished.

Not everyone who uses an architect makes this type of arrangement. Frankly, although it takes a big burden off the owner's shoulders, it is costly. Many people work with an architect on an hourly fee—usually around $20 an hour. You can, for example, pay an architect to do some rough plans which you can take to a builder who can detail them and carry on from there. You might want an architect to give his opinion on some stock plans you have bought or give you his feeling about an existing house you are interested in buying.

If you are going to use an architect for any extensive amount of work, have a frank talk with him about money. Unless he knows exactly how much you are prepared to spend either on land, building a house, or remodeling one, he is working pretty much in the dark. The tales you hear about families who have gone to an architect to design a house for them and then found that the house was going to cost twice as much as they could afford are tales about people who never told the architect exactly how much money they were prepared to spend. Architects have a pretty good idea of local building costs, and if you tell your man that you only have $20,000 to spend, he won't design a house that will cost $40,000. Also talk to the architect about his fee. You should know in advance what his charge is going to be. If he is working on an hourly rate, remember that each time he spends an hour with you, or in the office working on your project, his meter is running.

12 STYLES AND DESIGNS OF VACATION HOUSES

Vacation houses come in all shapes as well as sizes, and no one shape is perfect for every location, every site, or every family. A design that works well by the ocean may not be suitable for a snow area; a design that is fine on irregular terrain is not so hot if you set it on a flat piece of ground. And a design that suits one family may not fit another family nearly as well. All this is probably for the good. Our landscape would be even more depressing than it is if every vacation area were dotted with houses each one exactly like the other.

THE ONE-STORY HOUSE

This is probably the most common kind of vacation house. It is not the least expensive to build, however, and requires the most land per square foot of interior living space. It is also probably the most difficult kind of house to design well, for in a rather limited amount of space it's necessary to provide separate areas for sleeping, living, enter-

taining, and cooking, and at the same time achieve a good
traffic pattern through the house. And naturally, the smaller
the house, the more care must be exercised in planning the
interior space. One-story houses do best on relatively large lots
so that there is a degree of privacy from adjoining houses.
Many people prefer them because there are no stairs to climb,
it's possible to have access to the outdoors from bedrooms as
well as living areas, and they are relatively easy to maintain.
Unless expansion is planned for in advance, however, they are
rather difficult and costly to add to, when and if additional
space is required.

THE TWO-STORY HOUSE

This style, of course, gives you the
most amount of living space for the money. A two-story house
doesn't have to be as carefully planned as a one-story house
because most of the bedrooms are on the second floor and completely separate from the living and cooking areas. You can put
a two-story house on a relatively small lot and still have a sense
of privacy in the upstairs bedrooms. A two-story house can be
an ideal solution when there is an attractive view that cannot
be fully appreciated from the ground floor. It is a simple matter
—and not much more expensive—to reverse matters and put
the living and cooking areas on the second floor and the bedrooms on the level without the view. If you want to start out
relatively small but be able to expand in the future, a two-story
house makes a good deal of sense. You can finish off the first
floor and leave the second one unfinished until you need it or
have the money to do the work. Even an unfinished second story
can be used as a sleeping area. A two-story house can be great
if you have a lot of kids. You can stick them upstairs and if their
rooms are always a mess and the beds never get made it won't
make any difference—you can always stay on the first floor. We

know of one family with five children who live happily all summer in a two-story house. The kids sleep in two dormitories upstairs and their mother goes upstairs only twice during the entire vacation season: once in the early summer to see that everything is OK and once when the house is being closed up, to give the place a good cleaning. The rest of the time she enjoys life—downstairs.

Of course, a two-story house is not perfect. Stairs can be a big drawback, although climbing stairs isn't bad for you if you are healthy. But the compulsive housewife who runs up and down stairs a hundred times a day will get tired. Also, a two-story house is somewhat more difficult to maintain on the outside—painting, washing windows, and so forth. And there is no easy access to the outdoors from the upstairs bedrooms. But, just the same, a two-story house can make a dandy vacation house, especially for a large family.

THE SPLIT-LEVEL

These are also called "multilevel" houses, and they are a cross between a one-story and two-story house with some of the advantages and disadvantages of each. There are stairs, but they are relatively short flights; and while you can climb as many individual steps a day in a split-level as in a two-story, the fact that the flights are short seems easier for most people. A split-level is somewhat less expensive to build —all things being equal—than a one-story with an equal amount of space, but it is not as inexpensive as a two-story.

You can get good separation of sleeping and living areas in this kind of house, and there are all sorts of ways to arrange them. You can have the bedrooms on the upper level or you can use it for the living area and put the bedrooms on the lower level. You can toss the kitchen in the middle so that it works pretty well for either indoor or outdoor eating. It's a flexible sort of house that tries to be accommodating. The lower level can be opened up with sliding glass doors to provide easy access to a terrace or the outdoors.

A split-level doesn't require much design talent to make the interior work, but the exterior often turns out to be rather depressing. A split-level or multilevel house does best when set into a slope in the land. This is the kind of site for which it was originally designed. When it is set on a flat piece of ground, it generally looks out of place. And it's not an economical design when soil conditions are such that it becomes expensive to excavate for the lower level or when there is a moisture problem so that the below-grade areas are damp or require extensive treatment to make them water-and damp-proof.

THE A-FRAME

A few years back it looked almost as if the whole country might be covered with this kind of house, but happily it has lost some of its appeal, except in certain areas where it belongs. The A-frame house looks like the capital letter *A* with the roof and walls combined into a single plane. It was originally designed for a specific purpose—as a moderate-cost vacation house in ski country where snow accumulations are heavy. Because of its design, the roof sheds snow like a duck sheds water and the house can therefore be framed with relatively light materials as compared with a conventional house which has to have a roof reinforced at extra cost to withstand the weight of the snow. The first A-frames were simple affairs with solid sides and doors and windows only at the ends. This was a pretty inexpensive house to build and was a favorite of do-it-yourselfers because it was also an uncomplicated house to build. But bit by bit it got fancier and fancier. Dormers were added to the sides to provide more light and usable space, the overall size was increased to provide a second floor—and pretty soon it had become a rather expensive proposition.

As a basic design, the A-frame has a lot of drawbacks. First, only a portion of the interior space is usable for living, and there is even less usable space on the upper floor than the lower one. Unless dormers are cut into the sides, there is no cross ventilation—you get air either from the front or rear. This is no problem if the house is going to be used for skiing, but as a summer place in a warm climate it's a definite drawback. It is not a particularly good design to use near the seashore or anywhere else where strong winds occur. Unless the house is firmly anchored to its foundations, it can be blown over in gale-force winds. All the same, for its original purpose—a simple and inexpensive ski house in an area of heavy snow—it's a very practical design.

LOG CABINS

There are two types of log cabins, or rather, log houses. One is the more or less traditional cabin that lots of people find pretty old hat. Nevertheless, they can make a comfortable and inexpensive vacation house in the right location. The right location, of course, is in the woods. Put an ordinary log cabin by the seashore or in the middle of a flat field and it will look out of place. But nestle it in a forest or by the side of a lake and it does just fine. The other kind of log cabin has a very contemporary look—in fact, the logs are sometimes set vertically rather than horizontally. This kind of log cabin or house does very well in any location.

Log cabins and log houses built today are made from precut logs. There is no wall framework—the logs provide all the necessary structural support as well as exterior and interior wall surfaces. Most logs used are around four inches thick and furnish sufficient insulating qualities so that, except in very cold areas, no other wall insulation is required. The logs are made of cedar or some other durable softwood, and they require little if any maintenance. Give them a coat of penetrating exterior stain or sealer now and then and that's about all that's needed.

Log houses come in a wide variety of sizes. You can get a tiny little one-story job that's just right for one or two people, or as a starter house. You can get a two-story log house that can accommodate a good-size family plus guests.

The typical log cabin isn't accepted everywhere. Many planned communities don't allow them at all while others allow only those of more contemporary design. This type of house is usually manufactured and shipped precut. A lot of outfits are making them and you'll find manufacturers in almost every area—Northwest, Southwest, Midwest, South, and Northeast. They are one of the best buys for the money in the vacation-house field.

CHALETS

Like the log cabin and the A-frame, this is a specialized design that does fine in the mountains where it originated. It is basically a large house—usually two stories—and a rather expensive one to build because the design is complicated. We prefer the ones that have been pretty well stripped of the gingerbread—we don't think it's that attractive and it adds a lot to the cost.

BARN HOUSES

These are houses designed and built to resemble remodeled barns. They have a pleasant informal appearance combining traditional with contemporary design. They are not particularly inexpensive to build, but they do provide a lot of interior living space. They do well by the shore or on a lake but look a little out of place on the side of a ski slope. At least we think they do.

TRADITIONAL, CONTEMPORARY OR MODERN

The style of vacation house you select depends on your individual taste, of course, but it can also be affected by the location of the house and your budget.

By and large, the most expensive to build is the traditional. By traditional we mean California ranch, Cape Cod, saltbox, colonial, Florida Spanish, and similar styles. All of these designs originated in those dear dead days when materials were scarce but labor was dirt cheap, and to build a traditional house today still requires more labor than some of the other designs. It's hard to place a traditional house on a problem lot, and it's hard (and often impossible) to modify the plan to meet special requirements and still retain the traditional character of the house. If you want to shield the front of a house from a busy street, for example, you can put up a contemporary or modern house with a solid or almost-solid front, but if you try to take the front windows out of a Cape Cod or California ranch, you are going to end up with a pretty strange-looking house.

Traditional is a safe design for a house. It's an easy house to sell or rent, and this makes it an easy house to finance. In many vacation areas it is almost the only acceptable design— you will get some pretty hard looks if you build anything but a Cape Cod house on Cape Cod.

It's hard to explain just what a "contemporary house" is. Let's simply say it's a cross between a traditional and a modern house. The exterior design lends itself to countless variations and the interior floor plan is more flexible and open than that usually found in a traditional house. It is a very popular design for vacation houses, and you'll find it in planned vacation communities as well as in manufactured houses—precut, prefab, or modular.

A modern house is usually one designed by an architect to suit a particular family's requirements. It is often designed to fit a particular site as well. It is an uncluttered house, often with a rather severe exterior. Because there are no restrictions on the design, it is the most flexible of all and the best suited to take full advantage of a particular site or view. Depending on what goes into it, it can be the most expensive or the least expensive house to build. As it usually has a somewhat far-out appearance and is designed to meet the taste requirements of an individual or a family, rather than of the masses, it can be a hard house to sell or even rent. This is especially true if the house is built in an area where the popular taste is toward the traditional. We knew of one rather weird-looking modern house that was on the market for several years. In spite of the fact that the price kept going down, it didn't attract much interest because it looked so out of place among the more traditional vacation houses in the area.

But if you don't expect to have to sell, or you don't mind taking a loss or not making a profit if you do sell, a modern house can be great—if it's a good house to begin with. One of the things we don't like about many modern vacation houses is that they appear to have been designed more to allow the architect to experiment with new ideas and with little appreciation for the environment or even the requirements of the family that is paying for the house. These "conversation houses" as we call them can be as much a blot on the landscape as a bunch of mobile homes or an industrial plant. If you decide to go for modern, see that the designer respects the land as well as your needs.

13

SKI, WATERFRONT, AND DESERT HOUSES

Where you decide to build your vacation house will influence the particular piece of land you select as well as the design of the house. When you look at waterfront property, there are certain vital things to consider. Equally vital but different questions arise when you look for a lot for a ski house or desert house. The same holds true of house design and construction. A design that makes a perfect waterfront or beach house can not only be unsuitable for the mountains but can even be a disaster. This does not mean that some designs can't be used anywhere, because some can and are. But, by and large, it's best to stick to a house that has been designed to meet a particular environment.

THE SKI HOUSE

Now we are talking about the mountains, and as far as the land goes you should look for something at the bottom of a slope where there will be plenty of sunshine in fair weather. It should have good natural drainage so that when the spring thaws come, the area around the house won't be flooded. Don't buy land *on* a slope. Hillsides are not only costly to build on and to reach when the roads are covered with snow, but you'll also be troubled in the spring when the snow melts and sends torrents of water downslope. Slope sites are to be avoided especially when a lot of house building is going on above you. It often happens that so many trees are removed that nothing is left to hold the thin layer of topsoil. Water, rocks, and dirt will come rushing down towards your house to herald the coming of spring.

You want a site that offers as much protection from wind as possible. Don't buy land at the end of a natural funnel, for it can keep your house in a deep freeze all winter long. Look for a site that will allow you to set the house in such a position that the living areas with the large amount of glass can face west and get the warm afternoon sun.

Remove trees from the immediate area of the house so that the sun can reach it. But don't take out any more trees than necessary. Aside from the fact that they keep the topsoil in place, trees can also provide a good wind protection to the house and to you.

A mountain ski house must be designed inside and out to deal with heavy snows and water resulting from melting snow. A roof with a steep pitch is good; it will shed snow readily and therefore doesn't have to be framed with extra heavy timbers. This is why the A-frame design is so popular as a ski house. The disadvantage of the steep roof, however, is that snow sliding off it accumulates along the sides of the house and can eventually pile up to block the first-floor windows. Worse, when the snow melts the water can leak through the windows into the house unless the windows are watertight. Some designers of ski houses favor a roof with so little pitch that it is almost flat. A roof of this kind must be heavily framed to handle the snow load, but the thick blanket of snow does act as insulation, helping to keep the house warm, and there is no problem with large accumulations of snow sliding off the roof and piling up on the ground.

In areas where snow accumulations are heavy, the entrance doors and first-floor windows should be set higher than normally so they won't be obstructed by the snow. Entrance doors should be protected on the outside either by the overhang of the roof or by a shed. It's a good idea to have a storm entrance or mud room right off the entry so that skiers can shed their boots and outerwear before coming inside.

Skiers like high ceilings. They can carry their skis indoors to wax them or adjust the harness. The first floor requires a covering that won't be harmed by water and won't be easily scratched. Stone, brick, and slate are excellent, but vinyl or wood with a durable water and scratchproof finish are also fine.

Don't skimp on essentials when building a ski house. It should be good and tight with plenty of insulation in walls, roof, and even under the floor to keep the house warm and cut down heating costs. Use the best-quality wood windows you can afford. The same holds true for doors. Be sure that windows and other glass areas are either made of insulating glass or have storm windows to cut down heat loss. Even if you don't worry about heating costs, you'll want windows and glass areas that won't be uncomfortably cold when you sit near them. If the house is tightly built, it can be heated relatively easily and for a moderate cost even in the coldest weather. Many ski houses don't even have central heating but depend on the fireplace and a few electric wall or room heaters to keep them warm.

It's wise to build or buy a ski house from people familiar with local conditions. What can be considered a heavy snow in some sections of the country is looked upon in others as nothing more than a heavy frost. If you plan to build from stock plans or to put up a manufactured house, have the plans and specifications checked by the local building inspector to make sure that they conform to local regulations. It's worth the small cost to have a local architect check them over as well. He may be able to suggest minor changes that would make the house more suitable for that particular area and its local conditions.

THE WATERFRONT HOUSE

The main consideration in selecting a waterfront site, whether it is on a lake, river, bay, gulf, or ocean, is to get a location where the house will be safe from high water. Lakes, ponds, and even quiet little brooks can overflow their banks at certain times of the year, and while the damage to the house may be slight compared to what can happen when the ocean acts up, there will still be a lot of damage if water gets into the house. This type of water damage is something not ordinarily covered by a homeowner's insurance policy, either. And even if the house itself is not harmed by rising water, the grounds may be covered with mud, the well polluted, and the septic system flooded. Last but not least, if you are going to try and get a mortgage loan to build your house, no lender will be anxious to advance you money if he suspects that one fine day your house may be washed away.

The best arrangement is to have a site that is deep or high enough so that the house and grounds will be perfectly safe from water no matter what happens. With ocean property or a site on the Great Lakes, you can get a pretty good idea of prevailing local conditions by talking to the Coast Guard. Or you can talk to the local building inspector, the county agent, and even a local banker. In questionable areas, the house can be protected by a seawall or bulkhead, but these can be very expensive, running as much as $100 per foot. We know of a $25,000 vacation house with a $55,000 seawall. In the case of a beach house, sand dunes offer pretty fair protection if they are high enough and covered with enough vegetation so they won't be blown away by the winds. Setting snow fences along the dunes will help preserve them, but there is nothing like natural vegetation to hold the sand in place.

When it is not possible to make the house perfectly safe from the water, select a design that will prevent damage to the house if the land around it is submerged. One approach is to set the house on high piers so that water can wash under it without doing any harm. This is a popular approach for beach houses and has the further advantage of getting the house high enough so that there is a view over the tops of dunes or even another house. In some houses the area under the house is enclosed with flooring and siding but with a space left between each board so that water can flow in and out without doing any harm. This area provides a good place for storage or for dressing rooms.

Because waterfront property is the most expensive of all, lots are usually small with the houses set close together. This being the case, you want a design that will give you the maximum amount of privacy from your neighbors, and at the same time allow you to enjoy your waterfront view. A contemporary or modern design works best here. Windows can be eliminated in some cases or set high along the walls to provide ventilation and light without loss of privacy. An atrium design in which an outdoor area is enclosed on three sides by the house is another good solution: you can still have your view of the water but be completely private.

Dampness can be a problem, so even if the house is to be used only in summer have a fireplace or some kind of heater to dry the place out when necessary. Strong winds are a problem if the house is on a large body of water. Use wood shingles or the seal-down type of asphalt shingles on the roof, and try not to require awnings and other exterior items that can be blown away by high winds. If the house is on a sandy beach, don't use paint on the outside walls: wind-driven sand is like sandpaper and wears off the paint rapidly. Coat the wood with a stain or bleaching oil or just let it weather naturally.

THE DESERT HOUSE

Don't buy a building site too close to irrigated farmland. All that green may look pretty but it can make the area uncomfortably humid. Try to find a site where your view or outdoor living area faces south or east rather than west. A western exposure, even when partially blocked by a ridge or distant mountains can be uncomfortably hot in the afternoon. Watch out for sites set along canyons and ravines. These are often attractive but they can be a problem. If there is no vegetation you may get road washouts when there is a cloudburst, and if there is vegetation all around you, you may get a nasty brush fire during a dry spell.

A good desert house has to be rather specialized because it must be cool during the day and warm in the evenings. Even in winter you'll find that days on the desert can be pretty warm while nights are quite frigid. The house should really be air conditioned. It also needs plenty of insulation in walls and roof—essential whether you air-condition or not. Unless you can afford the rather expensive heat-absorbing glass, use a minimum amount of glass on the west side of the house. Incidentially, insulating glass is effective in preventing heat loss from the house but it does not keep outside heat from entering the house. Only the heat-absorbing glass or a special coating over regular glass does that trick.

The best-style house is one with a roof that has a good wide overhang. This will shade the house from the sun. The roof line can be extended to provide shades for outdoor living areas as well. White roofing is good because it reflects the sun's heat away from the house whereas a black roof absorbs heat and makes the house that much warmer.

A masonry house is most practical for the desert. Adobe or masonry block walls will provide good insulation, making the house cool in hot weather and easy to heat in cold. Because the air is dry, you won't have any problem with condensation on the inside of masonry walls and therefore they can be left exposed and just given a coat of paint.

As far as design goes, it's hard to beat the atrium used by the early Spanish settlers in our Southwest. The house was laid out as a quadrangle with a garden and court in the center.

Overhanging roofs provided shade so that one could walk outside from one area of the house to another without being exposed to the sun. Even in this age of air conditioning, this is a most practical arrangement. But it does require a lot of land.

14

THE BUILDER

This fellow is also called a general contractor. You'll need him if you are building your own vacation house or remodeling one, unless you plan to do the work yourself or act as your own contractor.

A builder is qualified and equipped to handle the entire building operation from clearing the land to putting the final coat of paint on the living room walls. Some builders operate big concerns and have qualified crews to handle all phases of the work. Most contractors, however, have their own crew do certain parts of the job and then "sub" out other parts of the work to specialized subcontractors. For example, a builder may have his own carpentry and masonry crew but farm out plumbing, wiring, and painting to subcontractors.

The success of any building project depends on the quality of the builder, so it's important to get the right one and at the right price. If you are working with a local architect, he can give you sound advice on the selection of a builder because he has probably worked with many contractors in the area. If you don't have an architect, you'll have to select the builder on your own. Which builder to use can sometimes be an academic problem in the back country—there may be only one around—but in most places you will have a choice to make.

There are two primary considerations involved in selecting a builder: how much is he going to charge, and how good is he?

Finding out how much a builder is going to charge, particularly for a new house, is easy—you just ask him to give you a bid on it. But before you can get a sensible bid you not only have to know what you want, but also have it worked out in precise detail. You should show the builder the site on which the house is to be put so he can determine what it will cost to clear the site and put in the foundations. Next, you need a complete set of plans for the house. Finally, you need a list of the materials you want to use. At this stage of the game, you may not have decided exactly what materials you want; if this is the case, you had better discuss the subject thoroughly with the builder before he makes his bid. What you use to build a house can have as much bearing on the final cost as the size or design. Decide what materials you are going to use for roofing, siding, windows, doors, flooring, interior walls and ceilings, kitchen cabinets, plumbing fixtures, sliding glass doors, and as many other items as possible. (How some of these materials compare in cost is discussed in Chapter 8, "How to Reduce Building Costs.") A qualified builder knows what he must charge per square foot of space so he can quickly give you a rough estimate on construction costs. If this estimate is far beyond your budget, tell him so. He can then suggest substitute materials that will help bring down the price of the house. But the builder must have all the necessary information about the house before he can make an intelligent bid, and you must give the same information to any builders who might be bidding on the job if you want to make an intelligent comparison between their bids.

The foregoing applies as much to a remodeling project as it does to new construction. Plenty of people have made the mistake of accepting the lowest bid only to find out later that the builder they chose planned to use the lowest-quality materials available, whereas the higher bids were based on using stuff of better quality. Everyone must bid on exactly the same thing if the bids are to make any sense.

Don't confuse a bid with an estimate. An estimate is just that—a guess as to what the job will cost. A bid, on the other hand, if it is in writing, is a more or less firm commitment as to what the job will cost. Bids *should* be in writing and should detail pretty much how the work is to be done and what materials are to be used.

The general rule is to try and get three bids on the job. This will give you a pretty fair idea of price range. Do not automatically take the lowest bid even if you are satisfied with the quality of the materials the bidder plans to use; there is more to selecting a builder than how much he is going to charge. You also want a builder who will do a good workmanlike job throughout, and one who will get started and finished in a reasonable length of time.

By and large, you won't have too much difficulty finding a good builder, especially if he has been in the business for a few years. It's always wise, however, to get from him the names of some people he has built homes for and to check with them as to his qualifications. There is not much point in checking out an established local builder with the Better Business Bureau or local chamber of commerce because these outfits don't worry overmuch about small matters. Finding a builder who is a paragon of responsibility is something else again. Your average local builder can be pretty exasperating at times. He'll start a job and work on it for a week or so and then disappear to do something else. This is especially the case if you are trying to get your house built during his busy season—spring, summer, and early fall. You are usually better off, timewise, if you can arrange it so he starts in late fall and has the winter and early spring to complete the job. These are the months when there isn't much demand on his time, and once he gets the house weathertight, he can finish the interior regardless of the weather.

After you have selected your builder, you should have an agreement drawn up between you detailing the work involved and the manner of payment. It's an awfully good idea to have this agreement examined by an attorney before you sign it. A lawyer can see that the agreement includes something to the effect that the builder has the necessary insurance so you can't be sued if one of his men gets hurt on the job, and that he will be responsible for any loss of materials once they are delivered to the site. There should be some provision in the agreement to protect you from a mechanic's lien in the event that the builder fails to pay the subcontractors or suppliers who furnished materials. The agreement should also be written so that when the work is finished, if any areas are not satisfactory to you, a certain amount of the final payment to the builder will be held in escrow until the matter has been settled to your satisfaction.

The usual method of payment is to make a partial payment after a certain amount of the work has been done, perhaps another payment later on, and the final payment when the work is completed satisfactorily. If you are using a construction mortgage loan to finance the work, the lender will not advance you money until he has inspected the work and finds it satisfactory. *Never* pay a builder money before he has done an amount of work to justify it.

When the job is finished and you get the final bills, take the time to make a complete inspection of the job. First, make sure that everything specified in the original agreement was completed in a proper manner. Open and close all doors, including kitchen cabinets, to make sure they open easily and latch properly when closed. Open and close all the windows to see that they work easily. Turn on the faucets of the plumbing fixtures to be sure that the drains work properly and have not become clogged with debris. Be on the lookout for minor flaws such as poorly fitted joints on interior trim, loose floor tile, electric wall switches that don't work, small areas on ceilings, walls, and woodwork that the painter missed, rough joints between sections of gypsum wallboard, and poorly fitted floor or wall warm-air registers. No matter how good the builder, there are bound to be a lot of minor flaws in every job.

Go over your agreement and see if certain items were omitted at your request. If they were, you should get a credit. On the other hand, if you added items you will be charged for these and the charge should be in line with the amount the builder told you they would cost.

After you have gone over the job carefully on your own, get hold of the builder and go over it with him. Point out those areas where you find the work unsatisfactory or where there is a discrepancy in the bill. Chances are he will make the necessary corrections and adjustments without much complaint. If he balks and you feel you are in the right, better consult with your attorney. You have an advantage in that you haven't paid the builder in full for his work, but he can slap a mechanic's lien on your property and eventually bring suit against you. Neither course makes a great start for a vacation house.

15

BEING
YOUR OWN
CONTRACTOR

You can save between 10 and 20 percent of the total cost of building or remodeling if you act as your own general contractor—provided all goes well on the job. Being your own contractor involves lining up the several subcontractors (called "subs") who will do the carpentry, plumbing, masonry, electrical work, heating, and roofing; setting up a schedule, and coordinating and supervising the work. All this takes a lot of time and effort which is why a general contractor gets paid as much as he does. It also takes a good deal of patience and understanding plus the ability to talk tough when it is required. You shouldn't even consider taking on the job unless you are going to be around to make decisions and deal with problems as they arise. And you certainly shouldn't consider taking it on if you know nothing about building, can't read or understand blueprints, or aren't really sure of what you want or how you want it done.

The job of being your own general contractor can be greatly simplified if you have a detailed set of plans to work from. The more phases of the work spelled out in drawings or in writing, the better. House plans drawn by your own architect are usually excellent in this respect as are many of the stock plans you can buy. Precut and shell houses are usually accompanied by

119

plans showing how the interior space can be arranged. In the case of a remodeling, it is worth a few hundred dollars to pay an architect or draftsman to put your ideas on paper.

You also need a complete list of the materials to be used on the project. Such a list should include all major items such as siding, roofing, type of plumbing fixtures, and kitchen cabinets. If you don't have the slightest idea what you need or what is available, discuss the matter with the sub involved. He may suggest only what he has, or has used previously, but in any event you'll know what you are getting and how much it will cost, and this is better than nothing.

WHERE TO BEGIN

Your first job as contractor is to line up people to do the work—the "mechanics" to use an old word for such artisans. Start with the best carpenter you can find. In the average house, carpentry is the biggest single item and one where the quality of workmanship counts most. Any mason can put up a foundation of concrete block that will look OK and hold up the house, and any licensed plumber can install a plumbing system that works. The same goes for an electrician —if he has a license, he can handle the job satisfactorily. But there is a great deal of difference between the amount and quality of work turned out between a really good carpenter and an average one. What's more, the good carpenter may be able to suggest some creative ideas that will not only make for a better house but even save you some money.

Another reason for starting out by finding a good carpenter is that he may be able to suggest men to do other portions of the work, such as masonry and plumbing. You are much better off working with a group of men who know one another and who have worked together on other jobs than working with a bunch of strangers. Men who have worked together in the past can coordinate a lot of the work without any supervision on your part. For example, the carpenter might call the plumber some evening and tell him that the house will be ready for rough plumbing by the beginning of the following week. This gives the plumber time to pick up the necessary materials and be ready to go to work right on schedule. If you are working with complete strangers—or worse, with people who don't like one another—you are going to have to plan a work schedule, try to maintain it, and perhaps take a financial loss if one workman is held up because someone else has not finished his end of the project.

You may also find that the carpenter can handle other jobs besides carpentry. Some carpenters, especially those in rural areas, are pretty much jacks-of-all-trades. They can do masonry, painting, even plumbing and wiring. This is all to the good. The fewer people involved in a job, the easier it goes; there will be fewer problems for you, and it will probably cost you less in the long run.

So start off with the carpenter and at least check in with the people he suggests for other phases of the work. And be as certain as you can that you and the carpenter are going to be able to get along. It doesn't make a great deal of difference if you don't particularly like the mason, plumber, or electrician. They will be in and out of the job pretty fast, and you won't have too much dealings with them. But the carpenter is going to be around throughout the job.

HOW TO FIND MECHANICS

The best way to locate good local mechanics is to ask around. In small communities everybody knows everybody else, and the man at the filling station or the grocery or the hardware store, or the lady who runs the local lunch counter, can probably give you some names of people to talk to. The local bank is a good source, and you can be pretty sure that the people they recommend at least have a good credit rating even if they may not be the best in their field as far as price and quality of work goes. Real estate brokers are another good source for names. If there is a local architect in town, check with him and see whom he recommends.

It's good if you can get the names of several men for each phase of the work, but this isn't always possible in small communities. You will often find several carpenters in a single area, but only one plumber or electrician, and you either use him or find someone from another area. As soon as you do line up a likely mechanic, go over the plans with him and get an estimate, or better yet, a firm bid in writing.

ESTIMATES AND BIDS

There is a big difference between an estimate and a firm bid, and you had better understand what it is. An estimate is a guess as to what a job might cost. A firm written bid is exactly what it is going to cost. Estimates are easy to get because they don't mean very much. An electrician, for example, may estimate a job at $450, but when he submits his final bill it may be for $525. You ask him why the difference and he'll explain that the job required more materials and labor than he had figured. Chances are it was an honest mistake on his part, and you have to fork up the $525. But if he had given you a firm bid in writing for $450, *he* would have had to absorb the loss of $75. That's why it's hard to get a firm bid. You can get firm bids, of course, but usually only when you deal with a general contractor or a large outfit that has trained men who can accurately figure job cost and where the volume of work is large enough so that if they bid too low on one job, they can pick up the loss on the next one. A small outfit or a single individual can't afford to operate this way, so he prefers to give only estimates. On some work you can't even get an estimate. This is especially true with remodeling jobs, because there is no telling what problems will arise once they get underway.

Most individual mechanics operate on a "time plus materials" basis. This means they will be paid by the number of hours they put into the job plus the cost of the materials. You can order the materials direct and pay for them, or the mechanic can order and pay for them and then be reimbursed by you. This isn't a bad arrangement if you have a hardworking mechanic who puts in a full sixty minutes' work for each hour he charges. Also, you will pay less per hour dealing with an individual than you would if the mechanic worked for a general contractor. You may, for example, get a carpenter to work for $5.50 an hour, but if the carpenter worked for a general contractor, the contractor might charge you $8.00 an hour to cover his overhead.

The only way any mechanic can give you even a rough estimate on what a job will cost is to know what is involved. That's why it's not only important that you have detailed plans to show him but also that you can indicate the quality of materials to be used. For example, a roof covered with cedar shingles is going to cost a lot more than an asphalt shingle roof. If your carpenter or roofer makes his estimate on the basis of asphalt and then uses wood at your request, the change is going to jack up the final bill considerably. And this holds true right down the line—even to small items such as hardware and lighting fixtures. The more details you can pin down at the beginning, the more the estimate will reflect the true cost of the job.

METHOD OF PAYMENT

When you discuss the project with the various mechanics, determine a satisfactory method of payment. Most mechanics want to be paid with a fair degree of promptness; they aren't in a position to carry an unpaid bill for more than a month. Plumbers, electricians, and masons who can complete their work in a relatively short time usually submit a bill when their part of the work is done and expect payment within thirty days. Carpenters who are going to be on the job for weeks and even months may need partial payments from time to time. Some may even want to be paid every week. Get these financial matters worked out in advance and make arrangements to have the money when it is needed. If you don't, you may find that the carpenter has to stop work on your job to take on another job so he has enough money to live on.

Never pay anyone until a sufficient amount of work has been done to justify the payment. Some carpenters, for example, will ask for an advance so they can buy materials for your job. This usually means that the carpenter is in a financial jam and either doesn't have credit at the lumber yard or needs the money for some other purpose—to pay for materials on some previous job, perhaps. In this situation the best approach is to establish credit on your own with the lumber yard. Let the carpenter order the materials and have them charged to you. You may want to do this in any case. If you are acting as your own contractor, the lumber yard will usually give you a discount just as they would any volume buyer.

There is still another advantage to charging materials directly: you can eliminate the possibility of a mechanic's lien being put on your property by a lumber yard. What sometimes happens is that a carpenter will order materials for a job and collect the money from you to pay for them. Then he doesn't pay the lumber yard, and pretty soon they get mad. If the lumber yard can't collect from the carpenter, they can legally go after you, and you may end up having to pay for the materials twice—once when you gave the money to the carpenter and again when you gave the same amount to the lumber yard. This can also occur with any mechanic—electrician, plumber, etc., but it is most apt to occur with carpenters.

But, by and large, you'll find that the vast majority of men who build houses are honest and reasonable people and respected members of their community. And once you have put a crew together, the work should proceed more or less smoothly.

To help keep things running smoothly you should arrange to check on the job every day or so. The best time to make your visits is either the first thing in the morning or late in the afternoon before the workmen leave for the day. Making your inspections when work is in progress only slows things up. Also, it's best to establish a routine so that if problems arise that require a decision on your part, the men on the job will know when to expect you and not waste time trying to reach you by public telephone until a phone can be installed in the house.

One big mistake that amateur contractors make is changing their minds after something has been completed. This is upsetting to the men, and it is also expensive—you have paid to have it done one way, and will have to pay to have it undone and then done over again. The time to change your mind is when you are still working with plans—not after the work has been completed.

If you are going to supply certain materials for the job, be sure that they are on hand when needed. You can expect a lot of grumbling—not to mention extra charges—if work is held up because the special kind of vinyl flooring you were going to order hasn't arrived in time, or you forgot to pick up the automatic dishwasher you were going to buy at a discount house.

Decide which member of the family is going to handle the job and have this individual deal with the workmen. It can get very confusing if one day the man of the family is running the show and the next day the woman. It doesn't matter who takes on the role of contractor, but let it be one person and not two.

16

THE STICK-BUILT HOUSE

The term *stick-built* refers to conventional on-site construction, where the entire house is put together on the site—stick by stick—as opposed to the varying degrees of manufactured housing. Of course, this is a slight exaggeration. Usually some elements, such as windows, door frames, kitchen cabinets, and so forth, are factory assembled and delivered to the site ready for installation. But even so, the major portion of the house is put together board by board.

A stick-built house can be any kind of house—traditional, contemporary, or modern. It can be a one-room shack you build yourself or a twenty-room vacation mansion. It is a method used to build entire vacation developments and it is also used for individual custom housing.

Unless you are going to build the house yourself, a stick-built house is usually the most expensive to build or to buy on a square-feet basis. This holds true whether it is an individual house or one in a development. The reason for this is the amount of labor required on the site to cut and assemble the thousands of pieces it takes to build even a modest-size house. It also takes more time to build a stick-built house than any other kind. The average builder needs a couple of months to

126

complete even a modest vacation house, and if it is a large and complicated house, the work may simply drag on. Until the shell of the house is complete, bad weather can often delay the work.

Stick-built construction gives you the widest latitude in the selection of materials. When you buy any kind of manufactured house, you get what the manufacturer provides, but with a stick-built house you can specify exactly what you want from the grade of lumber used to frame the house to the design of the wood molding used for interior trim. It is also the most flexible method of construction and often the only practical method for certain vacation houses—a very modern house, for example—where precut or panelized construction would be impractical.

But by the same token, a stick-built house involves more unknown factors than any other type of construction. Unless you are familiar with the quality of the work your contractor does, you can't be sure just how well he'll do the job until the house is finished. Then it's usually too late to do much about sloppy workmanship. And unless you have very detailed plans and specifications, you won't know exactly what you will get until the house is finished. If an architect is handling the job, it's a different matter. He can help you select a contractor who does good work and he can supervise the work so that it is done in accordance with his plans and specifications.

If you are building the house yourself, with your own two hands, the situation is somewhat different. In this case stick-built construction is the least expensive type because you are supplying all the labor free. It will be less expensive than a shell, precut, panelized, or anything else on the market. When every dollar counts, and if you have the time and the skill, this is the type of construction to select.

17

SHELL HOUSES

If you want to swing a vacation house on a limited budget, if you'd like to do some but not all of the work yourself, or if you'd like to pay for a house out of current income, a shell house may be your answer.

A shell house is just that. A shell. It has four outside walls with windows and doors, a rough floor, and a roof. That's it. It isn't any particular style or type of house. For a relatively small amount of money you can have a shell house erected on your property by a dealer or manufacturer. If you want them to, some manufacturers will finish off the house almost completely, or you can finish it off any way you wish and in your own time. Obviously, the more work the manufacturer does, the more the shell will cost.

Shell houses started a long time ago as an answer to low-cost housing in rural areas—especially in the Southeast. Many farm families were living in crude shacks and couldn't afford to build or finance a conventional house. But they often owned their own land, and many of them were willing to finish off a house themselves once it was far enough along to provide them with shelter. So the concept of the shell house was born. The manufacturer or dealer put up the shell on the family's property and the family put up their land as security. The house was financed through the manufacturer, and while it was at a fairly high rate of interest, the payments were relatively low.

At one point, shell houses got a bad name because some dealers and manufacturers resorted to questionable financing tricks. This situation has been pretty well cleaned up, but even so, when you buy a shell—or anything else—read the sales agreement carefully if you are financing the purchase through the manufacturer.

The shell-house concept is ideal for vacation houses. In fact, one shell manufacturer claims he has produced more vacation houses than any other single outfit, and he is probably correct. A shell house is particularly well suited to the family that wants to save money by doing the work themselves. Building a house from scratch is a long, hard road, especially if you can work only weekends and during a too-short vacation. And framing a house, especially the roof, takes specialized knowledge. But if you buy a shell house, the heavy end of the work —the kind of work that often requires a couple of strong and experienced carpenters—is all done, and the family can live in the place while they go about the job of completing the house.

Shell houses are also good for the family that doesn't want to take on a long-term financial obligation and would prefer to pay for their vacation house out of current income—even if it takes a few years to do it. If you own your own land, you can buy a small shell house for $2,500 or so and a large one from around $4,000 up. Once it has been paid for, you can make improvements as you can afford them. It may take several years to complete the house, but you can camp in it while you work, and when it is finished you'll own it free and clear.

In the vacation-house field you'll find all types and styles of shell houses, and all sorts of variations on the original shell-house theme. There are log cabins assembled out of precut logs, Cape Cod cottages, A-frames, contemporary designs, traditional summer houses, and so forth. Some will be stick-built right on the site—board by board—just as would be the case with a conventionally built house. Some manufacturers use precut materials and some go for panelized construction or a modular unit. Some shells are made by large outfits with wide distribution; some are turned out by local concerns—often large lumber yards—and serve only their immediate area. Some individual contractors will even build a shell for you—to any design you wish.

But most shells originate with companies set up for this type of operation. As a result, you will have a wide selection of houses to choose from. Some offer a wider selection than others and some, naturally enough, have better designs. Some specialize in one particular kind of a house, such as a log cabin or A-frame. If you deal with one of the latter firms, you can get houses in different sizes, but they'll either be log cabins or A-frames, or whatever is the manufacturer's specialty.

FINDING A SHELL HOUSE

This is not always the easiest thing in the world to do, but the good old "yellow pages" are the first place to look. Check under "Contractors," "Builders," "Houses," and "Lumber Yards." Also try your local newspapers. Shell-house dealers and manufacturers who serve a particular area often advertise locally and also in regional magazines. Local real estate brokers, who usually know a lot of what's going on in the building field, may give you some leads as may the local chamber of commerce or local bank. A few shell-house manufacturers have national or almost-national distribution. Some of these offer a precut shell-house package that you put up; others work through a local dealer or contractor.

COST

Compared to a conventionally built house, the price of a shell house is pretty low. But this, of

SHELL AND PREFAB HOUSES

Shell House

Pacific Frontier Homes, Inc.,
Fort Bragg, California

Photo 1. An expandable redwood ranch house with sturdy post-and-beam construction. The original concept of this and other Frontier models came from the drawing board of Henrik Bull, AIA. Designed for low maintenance, economy, and durability along with a feeling that a vacation house should represent an exciting, warm, and pleasant refuge, Frontier models are precut of natural, rough-sawn unfinished wood—most of it California redwood. Interiors of this easily expandable ranch house are a relatively inexpensive grade of redwood (containing knots and sap) with the clear grade used for exterior siding. The house has a rustic, natural look both inside and out. Exterior siding has a cream and reddish-brown appearance which weathers to a soft grayish-tan or can be stained to achieve a one-color look. This model is available in two-, three- or four-bedroom packages. Price for this 1,136-square-foot four-bedroom, two-bath shell is $8,926 which includes all lumber, hardware, plywood, doors and windows, floor joists, roof deck, shingles, and porch decks. It does not include wiring or plumbing. Prices are FOB Fort Bragg. Delivery in California averages around $300 and runs up to $750 out of state, depending on mileage.

Photo 2. Living room is open to ceiling and exposed redwood beams. Clerestory windows at front afford both light and privacy while the opposite wall of sliding windows encompasses scenic view.

Photo 3. Deep overhang of roof pleasantly shades deck and living room while adding individuality to overall design. Heavy framing members of Frontier homes are precut, drilled, completely manufactured, numbered and keyed to drawings. They go together quickly, usually in a day or two, and from there on, carpentry work is not complicated. The manufacturer is refreshingly candid when he says, "although the simplicity of the system lends itself to a do-it-yourself approach, the construction is not instant or easy. Simple, yes—easy, no."

Floor Plan. Frontier I

1

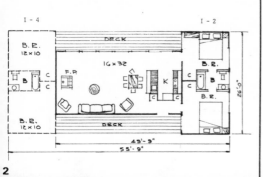

2

3

Shell House

Jim Walter Corporation, Tampa, Florida

An attractive, livable shell house on pilings, and one that can
be built on any terrain, *The Casual* can be erected in
twenty-nine states including most of the Southeast, as far west
as Arizona and Nevada, and north to New Jersey and New
York. This house and other Jim Walter models are stick-built on
your site. *The Casual* runs around $4,000 for the shell which
includes all exterior work finished but no interior finishing. An
almost-finished house runs to around $12,000 depending on
local labor rates. Jim Walter Homes offers financing to
qualified buyers. Base price includes two sliding glass doors
and sun deck. There is good storage space underneath the
house for a car or boat and the remaining space can be
screened or made into an additional room.

NOTE: Also see Kingston Kottage on the cover.

Prefabs

Bartoli and Brady Enterprises, Inc.
Winston-Salem, North Carolina

Photo 1. Unique prefabricated vacation house designed for any climate, the *Topsider* can be delivered ready for assembly anywhere in the United States, Canada, and throughout the Caribbean. *Topsider 101* is a two-bedroom, two-bathroom house with 800 square feet of living space on the main level and 100 square feet of heated utility space in the basement (plus at least 35 feet of storage space). The house package includes all components necessary to complete the house with exception of foundation materials, roof shingles, electric panel, rough plumbing, and water heater. Price FOB Yadkinville, North Carolina, is $13,043. This includes two complete bathrooms, custom kitchen cabinets with plastic laminate, eating bar, compartmented stainless steel sink, garbage disposal, lighting fixtures, preinstalled electric wall heaters, and floor-to-ceiling glass panels.

Photo 2. As adaptable to ski country as to shore or woods, *Topsider* can be placed on almost any kind of terrain because of its pedestal-base design consisting of a central steel column support with rigid bolted trusses. It is heated by five 2,400-watt fan-coil heaters on upper level and three on lower level. The design-manufacturers say that *Topsider* can support a maximum 50-pound-per-square-foot snow load and can withstand hurricane winds up to 140 miles per hour.

Photo 3. Floor-to-ceiling glass on all sides of the octagonally shaped structure gives unobstructed view from every part of the house. Occupants have the airy feeling of living in a tree or in the crow's nest of a ship, but not the feeling of confinement, as living room flows into open kitchen space. Free-standing fireplace and hearth are optional at extra cost, as is range, refrigerator, and dishwasher. Central air conditioning is also available as an option. An extra bedroom may be added, if desired, by enclosing the lower level of house. Identical companion units and a "Mini-Topsider" are also available if more space is needed.

Photo 4. Component parts of *Topsider* ready to be loaded into trailer truck. Freight charges are approximately 90 cents a mile. Once the concrete pedestal foundation has been poured, a crew of six can assemble a house in about ten working days. Estimated cost of construction is around $5,000 depending on geographical location and local labor costs.

1

2

3

4

course, is for the shell only. A lot of money still has to be spent on materials before the house is complete. A shell will run from $2,500 to $15,000 or more. In some areas, if you start with a shell only, it will take a sum about equal to the cost of the basic shell to finish your house. If you've paid $5,000 for the shell, the final cost of the complete house will be close to $10,000, assuming that you hire someone to do the work. If you do the work yourself, you can cut this figure about in half so that the complete house will cost around $7,500.

Before you can make much sense out of what a shell house is actually going to cost, you've got to know what you are getting for your money. Items that are never included in the price of a shell are wells, septic systems, roads, and other basic land improvements. Excavation and foundations are also not included. As to what the various manufacturers do offer, you'll find a wide variation. Some manufacturers provide a basic shell; you must put it up or find someone to put it up for you. Other concerns will send a representative to the site to help you get started, and still others will furnish expert help but at a charge of maybe $50 or $75 a day. With some, the basic price also covers the cost of erecting it on your site. The cost of shipping the house to the site also differs with manufacturers. Some include in the basic price shipping within a reasonable distance from the plant. Some charge extra for shipping. Many shell-house companies have two prices: one is the cost of the basic shell and the other is for the shell plus some of the materials that you'll need to finish it off. The only way to compare prices is to get all the costs of having the shell delivered to your site and put up.

HOW LONG DOES IT TAKE?

This depends on the type of shell. A panelized house that is put up by a trained crew with special equipment may take only a day or two to put up. A log cabin made of precut logs may take a couple of men the best part of a week to put together. And, naturally, with any house it takes a certain amount of time to put in the foundations—even if they are just wood or concrete piers.

JUDGING QUALITY

Some shell houses are not only better designed than others but also are made of better materials. You will naturally pay more for the better-quality house, but it's worth it in the long run unless all you want is a shack. The manufacturer's literature usually mentions many of the materials used. One key to quality is the weight of the roof shingles. They will frequently be asphalt shingles, and the better houses will have shingles that weight 250 pounds per square or more. Lightweight, 210-pound, shingles can be a sign of minimum quality. Except in the case of log cabins made of precut logs, the quality house will have sheathing as well as siding while the poorer one may have only siding. The size and spacing of the wall studding is another good indication of quality. You will have a much more solid wall if it is framed with 2 by 4s spaced 16 inches apart than if they are spaced 24 inches apart, or if 2 by 3s are used in place of the heavier 2 by 4s.

Don't buy a shell, if you can possibly help it, before either inspecting a model or visiting an existing house in your area. If you can't do either, at least check the plans and specifications with the local building inspector and see if you can get a reading on the reputation of the manufacturer or dealer from a local bank, chamber of commerce, or Better Business Bureau.

18

MANUFACTURED HOUSES

In a nation enchanted with the concept, advantages, and end result of mass production, it's only natural that we have tried—and are still trying—to turn out houses on assembly lines in the same way that we turn out automobiles, refrigerators, and color TV sets. And while a good deal of progress has been made to achieve the complete manufactured house, nothing in the housing field as yet compares with Henry Ford's classic Model T.

In this day and age it is still something of a surprise to find a large percentage of houses—vacation as well as year round—built in much the same manner as houses were built a hundred years ago. Truckloads of basic materials are brought to the site, and a crew of men cut and assemble thousands of pieces to create a house. It takes a tremendous amount of time and labor to complete even a modest house and, since much of the work has to be done outdoors, the weather can cause delays. For lots of reasons it is difficult if not impossible to ensure a high standard of quality.

The concept of the manufactured house is based on the use of machines rather than hand labor to do most if not all the assembly work required. And this method can without question produce a better house for less money than putting all the pieces together by hand—especially if the hands are expensive and not highly skilled. But with the exception of the mobile home, which is delivered to the site complete and ready for immediate occupancy, the other so-called manufactured houses are manufactured only to a degree—a varying degree depending on the type of house. Within this group we find pre-cut, panelized, prefab, and modular houses.

For several reasons, we don't now have—and may never have—a complete manufactured house. One problem is trans-portation. The maximum width that can be shipped on high-ways is 14 feet. Some states allow only 12 feet. This means that no matter how you slice it, the widest complete house you can move from factory to site is 14 feet. Now and then you may read or hear about complete houses being delivered to a site by heli-copter, and maybe someday this will solve the transportation problem, but right now it's pretty much a promotion gimmick and far too expensive for the average person. Local building codes are another problem. They vary so much around the country that it is presently impossible to design a complete house that will be acceptable to every state and commu-nity.

So with the exception of mobile homes—which are clas-sified as vehicles in many states and are therefore not subject to restrictive building codes—you will find no true or complete manufactured houses at this time. But even partially manufac-tured houses are usually less expensive than stick-built houses of the same size and quality. And manufactured houses can be put together in far less time.

Price is not the only advantage a manufactured house of good quality has over a stick-built one. Many manufactured houses are designed by fine architects, and the exterior appear-ance as well as the interior planning of the houses are far better than you sometimes find in houses put up by local builders or developers. The quality of materials and workmanship is bet-ter than you would get in the average vacation house, and you also know in advance exactly what you are going to get for your money—down to the last detail in many cases.

Needless to say, some manufactured houses are better than others in both design and quality. Don't ever buy a manufactured house just on the basis of the literature you receive from the manufacturer or dealer. Find out if there is a model or an existing house in your area and pay it a visit to see what you actually get. Even better, visit an occupied house and talk to the owners, for they can tell you much more about the house than you will ever learn from the salesman at a model house.

WHERE TO FIND THEM

By and large, the distribution range of manufactured houses is somewhat limited—and not merely because of local building codes. Transportation costs force most concerns to limit their distribution to a distance of around 500 miles from the factory—a day's drive for a truck. Some outfits, such as the manufacturers of precuts, ship by rail and have national distribution, and some very large outfits have a number of factories which increases their distribution range. But for the most part manufactured houses are regional and often reflect this fact in their design.

Some large outfits with wide distribution advertise in national magazines, especially the home and leisure books. Smaller local outfits advertise in local newspapers. Real estate brokers, bankers, and local chambers of commerce can usually give you the names of outfits that have built or distributed these houses in your area. You can also write to the Home Manufacturers Association in Washington, D.C., and they will send you a list of their members. Manufactured homes are sometimes sold direct from the manufacturer. In other cases they are sold through a local dealer who is often a builder and can handle the assembly of the unit.

THE PRECUT HOUSE

This is the simplest form of manufactured house. The basic framing elements of the house—walls, floors, roof—are precut in the factory and shipped to the site for assembly. As all these parts are precision-cut and fitted in advance, they can be assembled with a minimum amount of labor and in a relatively short time. Also, they can be assembled with relatively unskilled labor, for each piece is marked and detailed plans and instructions are provided on how the parts should be put together. The reduction of on-site labor can save you about 10 percent over the cost of a stick-built house.

Because they are manufacturing parts rather than a partially assembled house, precut manufacturers offer a greater range of house styles and sizes than any other type of house manufacturer. In the precut field you'll find log cabins in a wide range of sizes, barn houses, Swiss chalets, A-frames, conventional summer houses along with contemporary and modern houses. Prices can range from $900 for a small cabin to $50,000 or more for a spacious contemporary house.

What is included in the basic package differs with different manufacturers. Some provide only the precut materials for a basic shell—four walls, windows, outside doors, rough floor, and roof. Other manufacturers provide all the essential materials for a complete house.

There are also different arrangements for assembling the house. Some manufacturers have their own crews, some rely on local dealers to put the pieces together, some have local contractors who are qualified to handle the job, and some leave it up to you to find a contractor. Many of the smaller units are designed for the do-it-yourself market.

Precut houses usually have the widest distribution range of all manufactured houses. This is so because the package of precut lumber and other materials can be shipped by train or truck at little more than it would cost to ship an equal amount of uncut lumber. Also, because the precut house does not include wiring, plumbing, and heating, the manufacturer doesn't have the problem of trying to conform to local building codes. A precut house is especially good if:

1. You are planning to build a house yourself. The smaller precut houses designed for the do-it-yourself market are a great deal easier and faster to assemble than a conventional stick-built house.

2. You are building in an area where there is a shortage of skilled labor. Even if the manufacturer or dealer does not have his own crew, you have a better chance of getting a satisfactory job done by the available labor than if you had them build a conventional house.

3. You are building in a remote area where building materials are rather limited or must be shipped a great distance.

4. You are looking for a design and plan superior to any you've been able to find in stock plans or from a local builder or developer.

Before you purchase a precut house, find the answers to some important questions.

Exactly how much do you get for your money and how much extra will it cost to complete the house? We cannot overemphasize the point that there is a wide range in what different manufacturers include in the basic package. A basic house selling for around $8,000 may come to $25,000 or more after you have put in the foundations, plumbing, wiring, heating, a fireplace, and other essential items. If the manufacturer or dealer cannot give you these figures, get an estimate from a contractor on what it will cost to complete the house before you buy.

Does the price for the house include shipping to your site? If it doesn't, how much will this cost? Also, who is going to put up the house? If the manufacturer does it, is this cost included in the basic price of the house? If it's an extra charge, how much? If you are going to have to get your own contractor to put the house up, get a bid from him on what this will cost.

How long will it take to get delivery?   One of the advantages of a precut house is that it goes up in a hurry, but if you have to wait months for delivery, you've lost this advantage—and maybe your summer vacation.

As we said before, you won't save a fortune building a precut house as opposed to a stick-built one—you may save only 10 percent. But if you buy your precut from a good outfit, you'll get a better house in less time with this method than with conventional construction.

PANELIZED HOUSES

This is the next step beyond the precut. Here, parts are not only precut on an assembly-line basis but are also fastened together in panels or sections. These panels are not as complete as you will find in a prefab or modular house. They may just consist of the frame or, in the case of outside wall sections, the frame covered on the outside with sheathing or siding. The panels are hauled to the site and then put together in much the same fashion as in conventional construction.

Panelization is usually done by local outfits—often lumber yards and building-supply houses. Some have stock plans of houses for which they supply the essential panels, or they can take your house plans and engineer them so they lend themselves to panel construction. Not every house, of course, is suitable for this type of construction. It seems best for somewhat conventionally designed houses rather than the more contemporary jobs.

Sometimes the outfit that makes the panels will put them together on the site; sometimes you must do this yourself or have it done by your own contractor. There can be a saving of up to 15 percent on this method of construction because the panels can be put together on an assembly-line basis. The

MANUFACTURED HOUSES

The Precut House

Lindal Cedar Homes,
Seattle, Washington

Photo 1. High gull-wing roof, extensive use of glass, and a conveniently livable floor plan combine to make this precut house, the *Riviera*, one of the more popular packages sold by Lindal Cedar Homes. In kiln-dried cedar this 1,187-square-foot three-bedroom, two-bath house sells for $10,940 in Lindal's "plus" category, which includes insulation. In the "standard" category, uninsulated, the package is $9,870. Lindal also precuts this and other models in Ponderosa pine, which sell for around $1,700 less in each category. Prices include nails, locks, hinges, aluminum windows, sheet glass, and roof shingles. Prices do *not* include masonry, foundation piers, plumbing, heating, wiring, or cabinets. All structural components are cut to exact length and numbered at factories, with the exception of a few of the difficult-to-assemble parts of the house such as gables, which are prefabbed. All prices are FOB Lindal factories, which are located in Tacoma, Washington, Schererville, Indiana, and New Westminster, British Columbia. For do-it-yourselfers, Lindal provides detailed construction plans well in advance of shipment so that subcontractors for heating, wiring, and plumbing may be lined up and the foundation laid. They also send a comprehensive, fully illustrated manual.

Photo 2. The *Sea Breeze*, a four-bedroom house with additional 21-foot loft area. The attractive contemporary styling is adaptable to either shore or wooded area. The two-story 1,784-square-foot house sells, in the cedar "plus" category for $14,960. Deck is optional. *NOTE:* Thatched area indicates loft.

1

Floor Plan 1.
Riviera.

BEDROOM
10-8 x 11-C

BATH

MASTER BEDROOM
10-8 x 15-0

CLO.   CLO.

CLO.

BATH

BEDROOM
10-8 x 10-0

CLOSET   LIN

UTILITY

KITCHEN
10-8 x 8-4

LIVING ROOM
17-2 x 16-0

BAR

DINING ROOM
10-8 x 8-0

5-0

5-0

16-0

8-0

8-0

DECK
(optional)

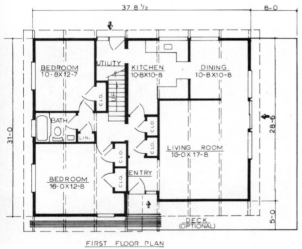

Floor Plan 2.
Sea Breeze

FIRST FLOOR PLAN

- 37 8 ½
- 8-0
- BEDROOM 10-8X12-7
- UTILITY
- KITCHEN 10-8X10-8
- DINING 10-8X10-8
- BATH
- LIN.
- CLO.
- CLO.
- CLO.
- CLO.
- CLO.
- LIVING ROOM 16-0 X 17-8
- BEDROOM 16-0X12-8
- ENTRY
- CLO.
- 31-0
- 28-6
- 5-0
- DECK (OPTIONAL)

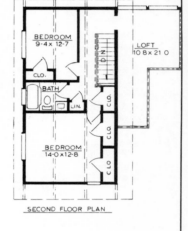

SECOND FLOOR PLAN

- BEDROOM 9-4 x 12-7
- LOFT 10 8 x 21 0
- BATH
- LIN.
- CLO.
- CLO.
- CLO.
- CLO.
- BEDROOM 14-0 x12-8

2

Log House
Boyne Falls Log Homes,
Boyne Falls, Michigan

Photo 1. Vertical log home of northern Michigan white cedar full half-logs, comes precut. This four-bedroom two-bath contemporary house *(Model 441)* can be built complete with plumbing, wiring, and heating on owner's foundation for $19,900 within a 50-mile radius of the plant. Beyond that radius, the house can be built for $16,900 on owner's foundation, less plumbing, wiring, and heating. Delivery charges up to a 1,000-mile radius run from $300 to $800.

Cedar, traditionally associated with the log cabin, combines strength, lightness, and long life. It is resistant to insects and weather. This company uses cedar exclusively in vertical log, horizontal log, and plank homes. The horizontal construction is somewhat more expensive but the 5-inch and 6-inch-thick log walls do not require further insulation and are suitable for year-round living anywhere in the United States. The vertical construction, with average 3-inch-thick half-logs, is primarily for vacation homes, but houses can be winterized at a reasonable extra charge. The company has many other models of log homes starting at around $3,895.

Photo 2. Log rafters and catwalk give authentic feeling to interior. Fireplace and cupboards are not included in package price.

Floor Plan. All models can be made longer or wider if buyer wishes. Charges usually run around $10 per square foot—about half that of a conventionally built house.

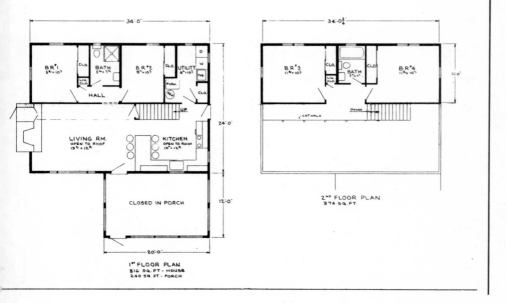

1ˢᵗ FLOOR PLAN
816 SQ. FT - HOUSE
240 SQ FT - PORCH

2ᴺᴰ FLOOR PLAN
374 SQ. FT.

Precut Log Cabins

Ward Cabin Co.,
Houlton, Maine

Today's log cabin can be as simple or as luxurious as the buyer wishes. Most companies that make log buildings not only have standard models but also will custom-design to any style or size wanted. The Ward Cabin Co., manufacturer of the log houses shown, designs their packaged buildings for erection on any type of foundation—concrete block or masonry wall, slab or piers. Once the foundation is in, houses can be erected either by the do-it-yourselfer or a local contractor. As with most packaged houses, materials are precut and labeled, so that there is little cutting necessary on the job. Additional labor is required to place the roof purlins and tie-beams, but these pieces, too, are precut and framed to minimize erection time. Only regulation carpentry tools are required for construction.

Ward's cabins are made of solid northern white cedar logs averaging 4½ inches in thickness. They are tongue-and-grooved and have special grooves for the calking between them. The logs are pretreated with preservatives and said to be air and watertight when erected properly. The company also states that insulation other than the natural insulation of the solid logs is usually not necessary, except in the roof area if the cabin is to be used year round in colder climates. Ward's windows are wood, complete with weatherstripping and locks. Picture windows have fixed insulating glass in center and double-hung side units. Exterior doors are Z-braced and made from solid logs. Ward's supplies complete materials with hardware for interior partitions, including studding, choice of knotty pine or cedar panel for sheathing both sides of partitions and trim. Bath and kitchen fixtures and appliances are not included, nor are roof shingles. A Ward cabin can range from around $2,500 for the Allagash Camp to around $25,000 for the larger cabins, including carport.

Photo 1. A Ward custom cabin on slab foundation. Plan is similar to their *Monte Carlo* (see floor plan 1) design with four gables on each side of house. House has cathedral ceiling throughout living, dining, and kitchen areas. Bath and bedrooms on both sides of house ensure privacy for family and guests.

Photo 2. A recently completed Allagash Camp model from Ward's less expensive series. Plan is similar to floor plan 2, with two bedrooms and one bath. With the exception of more frequent joints in wall layup, exterior walls are the same as Ward's higher-grade buildings. Gables are of vertical logs in camp-grade series and must be cut on the job. No modification of plan is possible in this series.

Photo 3. Suspended walkway from bedroom area at one gable end to the other spans a spacious living room in this two-story model.

Photo 4. Typical kitchen finished in cedar. Dutch door is optional.

Photo 5. Detail of corner assembly, showing dovetail of logs and tongue-and-groove configuration.

1

Floor Plan 1. The Monte Carlo.
Designed for erection on slab foundation.

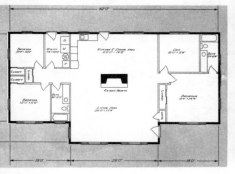

Floor Plan 2.
One of the plans in the Vacationer series.

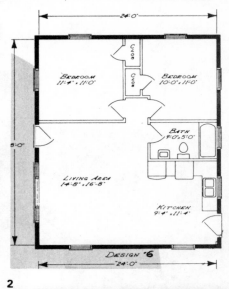

2

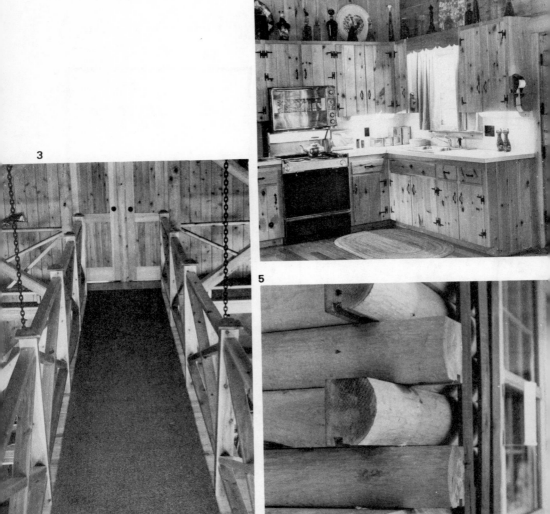

The Panelized House

*Acorn Structures, Inc.,
Concord, Massachusetts*

Photo 1. A traditional New England saltbox roofline gives this house a familiar homey look while interior floor plan and outside deck make it very much a part of today. Upper-level entry opens into a spacious 27 by 19 foot living-dining room with open kitchen. Generous use of glass at the front of house takes full advantage of the view, while the sloping ceiling on the opposite side of the living room adds a feeling of intimacy. Kitchen and large storage area is tucked into this wall as it slopes downward, convenient to living-dining area but not intrusive. Downstairs, three good-size bedrooms and 1½ baths can be entered from outdoors. House is available in finished form, complete with carpeting and fireplace, painted and trimmed throughout, for $21,893. Excavation, site, clearing, septic system, water and power are not included, nor is transportation, which is priced according to distance from Concord. Massachusetts. This and other Acorn models, which are shipped to building sites throughout the Northeast, may also be ordered in erected-shell stage (weathertight structures on specified foundation with studding partitions, insulation, stairs, and deck in place). Erected shell price on Salt Box 11 is $13,214. An intermediate choice, rough finish, which means brought to livable stage with plumbing, heating, electrical wiring, and kitchen installed, is $17,683 for this model.

Photo 2. Lower-level entry to bedrooms and to interior stairs leading to living-dining-kitchen areas. Special features may be incorporated into most Acorn houses to meet particular needs as long as variations are within the Acorn modular building system which includes 4-foot-wide wall panels and solid corner panels, which brace the structure.

Photographs: Sam Robbins

1

2

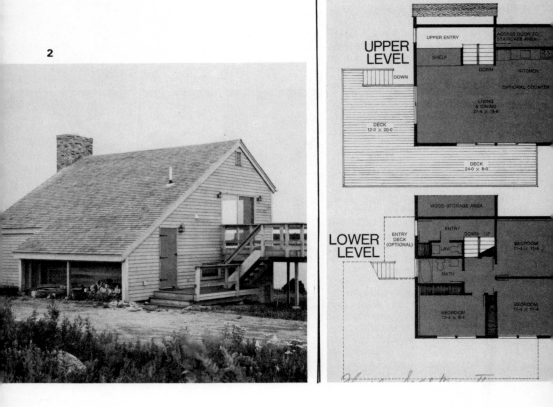

Floor Plan. New England Salt Box

UPPER
LEVEL

UPPER ENTRY

ACCESS DOOR TO
STAIRCASE AREA

SHELF

DOWN

KITCHEN

DOWN

OPTIONAL COUNTER

LIVING
& DINING
27-4 X 19-8

DECK
12-0 X 20-0

DECK
24-0 X 8-0

LOWER
LEVEL

WOOD STORAGE AREA

ENTRY

DOWN UP

BEDROOM
11-4 X 11-4

ENTRY
DECK
(OPTIONAL)

LAV.

BATH

BEDROOM
13-4 X 8-4

BEDROOM
11-4 X 11-4

The Precut and Panelized House

*Boise Cascade
Vacation House Division,
Lexington, Massachusetts*

Photo 1. Rough-sawn Philippine mahogany plywood with solid battens and unusual lines of wood-shingled roof combine rustic appearance and low maintenance with a comfortable and roomy interior.
The Hatteras has attractive features for both vacation and year-round living. Large living-dining area opens up to a spacious L-shaped balcony which can be used for extra sleeping area, playroom, or work area. Roof peaks to overhead skylight adding natural light to interior. The two bedrooms on the main floor are larger than usual and both have commodious closets. The master bedroom has its own bath-dressing room and the second bath is conveniently located near entry. Kitchen is compact and convenient to dining area. The price of the house, except for septic system and water supply, ranges from $23,000 to $29,000, depending on location and local labor costs. Component parts of the house are shipped in containerized packages anywhere the buyer desires. Arrangements are made for a representative of the company to be on hand to inspect the site and consult with local builder and contractor.
Photo 2. Living-dining-kitchen area opens onto balcony deck (optional). Interior walls can be finished with wallpaper, paint, or paneling. If a fireplace is desired, the company suggests a prefab metal type be used to avoid cluttering the simple roofline. One suggested way to treat chimney is to run it through skylight area.

1

Floor Plan. The Hatteras

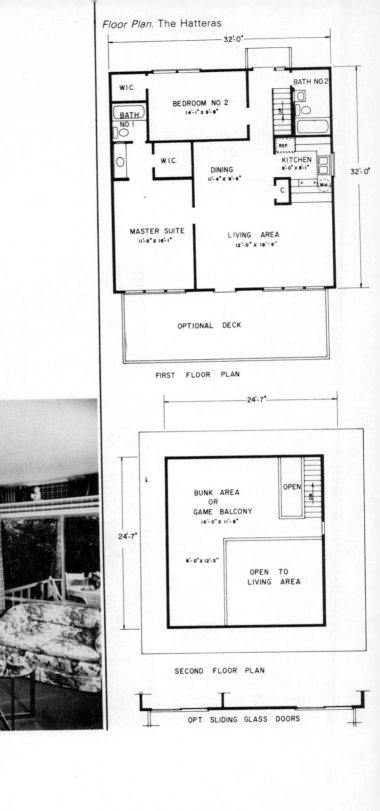

FIRST FLOOR PLAN

- 32'-0"
- W.I.C.
- BATH NO. 1
- BEDROOM NO. 2 14'-1" x 9'-8"
- BATH NO. 2
- W.I.C.
- REF.
- KITCHEN 8'-0" x 8'-1"
- DINING 11'-4" x 9'-6"
- C.
- W.H.
- MASTER SUITE 11'-8" x 16'-1"
- LIVING AREA 12'-0" x 19'-8"
- 32'-0"
- OPTIONAL DECK

SECOND FLOOR PLAN

- 24'-7"
- BUNK AREA OR GAME BALCONY 16'-0" x 11'-9"
- OPEN
- 8'-0" x 12'-3"
- OPEN TO LIVING AREA
- 24'-7"

OPT. SLIDING GLASS DOORS

2

The Package House

Stanmar, Inc., Sudbury, Massachusetts

Photo 1. Extensive decks and a screened porch add another 26 feet of living space to this comfortable two-bedroom-with-large-sleeping-loft leisure house. The ventilating clerestory windows under the broken roofline add interest to the exterior and bring light to the loft area. Called *Westwind*, this popular model is one of some forty designs by Stanmar, Inc. The costs of all structural and finish materials are fixed, with on-site construction costs varying according to locality. The average national price for the *Westwind* is $26,000 complete. Stanmar has sales centers located near major metropolitan and vacation resort areas in various sections of the country and in Puerto Rico, where full information about their homes is offered. The Stanmar package consists of basic materials necessary to construct and complete the structures, including nails, timber hangers, calking, and hardware. Exterior wall components are preengineered and preassembled in clear, kiln-dried rabbeted frames, dadoed together. Siding is rustic, grooved 5-ply mahogany veneer to be applied to 2 by 4 studs at 16 inches on center. Mahogany board-and-batten, cedar, white cedar shingles, or red cedar clapboards are optional at extra cost. Baked enamel aluminum windows include fiber-glass screens and self-storing storm windows. Fixed glass is insulated, calked, and beaded in place, including gable sections. Houses are plank-and-beam construction and the company states that all materials used are of the highest quality. Walls and floors are insulated when required. Decks are 2-by-6-construction-grade western red cedar. Interior walls are prefinished wood paneling in optional finishes or 1/2-inch gypsum wallboard. Kitchens include base and wall cabinets, countertop and stainless steel sink, with appliances and electric light fixtures by customer choice which may be included on an allowance basis. Builder specifications include American Standard or an equal middle-line of bathroom fixtures, with ceramic tile installed on three sides of tub, electric baseboard heating with individual thermostats and a 82-gallon electric hot-water heater. Kitchen and bathroom floors are covered with vinyl-asbestos tile and other floors are covered with finished oak unless carpet or other material is indicated. Not included in completion price are fireplaces, chimneys, septic systems, or landscaping.

Photo 2. Living room of *Westwind* showing extensive use of glass. Metal fireplace may be installed at extra cost. Outside deck railings and benches are included in package.

Photographs: James W. Brett

1

2

Floor Plan. Westwind.

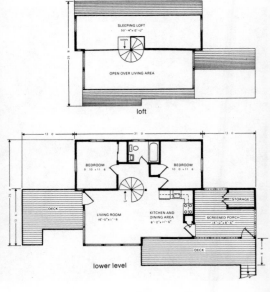

loft

lower level

The Precut Packaged House

American Timber Homes, Inc., Escanaba, Michigan

Photo 1. This rugged-looking year-round vacation house, *The Country Squire,* can be ordered with two or three bedrooms and one and a half or two baths. Shown here is the 26 by 48-foot, three-bedroom, two-bath model with cathedral ceiling. For those who appreciate natural, solid wood and like the feeling of solidity given by exposed trusses, these houses are singularly appealing. The roof systems are extremely sturdy and, according to the manufacturer, have been tested with loads equivalent to 8 feet of wet snow, making these houses particularly suitable, although not limited to, severe winter climates. All American Timber houses are of 2⅜-inch kiln-dried solid northern white cedar, a wood known for its durability and resistance to decay and insects. To further ensure these natural properties of cedar, these houses are also treated with a preservative. Exterior walls are rough-sawn, and unless desired, do not require paint or stain. They weather naturally to a silvery gray.

American Timber operates its own sawmill, factory, and kiln and delivers direct to home sites in most parts of the United States. The houses are designed on modules of 2 and 4 feet in width and 8 feet in length so that enlarging at a later day is no problem. Trusses, gable ends, and windows are factory assembled and the company's "Timber-Wall" construction members are cut to exact length. Covered porches, open decks, and enclosed terraces are included in the package and many different styles of exterior trim are offered. Not included are plumbing, heating, or wiring, but preliminary preparation is included. Package prices, running from around $4,000 to $35,000 do not, of course, include foundation or fireplace masonry. The company estimates that finished construction of their houses runs from 80 to 100 percent of the package price, with the average finished-construction price $25,000 to $30,000. They also have a custom plan service to design homes to individual needs.

Photo 2. Country Squire-Sportsman model shows roof system with dimensional trusses which can be substituted for log trusses if preferred. The dimensionals are western fir, cut and assembled in the company's plant. Windows are wood sash with screens. Bedroom and living area windows are glide-by or ventilating picture windows. Insulated windows are optional, but sliding glass doors are of insulated glass.

Photo 3. Swiss Chalet model is 24 by 32 feet on a full basement faced with fieldstone. Optional panel windows have been added to the upper front. Standard trim on all chalet models is Bavarian, but there is a wide choice of other decorative trims. All homes are designed with generous decks and porches. Chalets are available in two-, three-, or four-bedroom models with two baths optional. Prices on finished building range from $7,000 to $60,000.

1

Floor Plan 1. The Country Squire

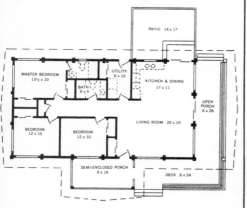

3

2

Floor Plan 2. The Swiss Chalet.

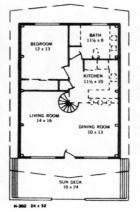

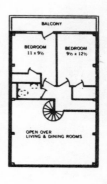

Modular Houses

Behring Corporation, Fort Lauderdale, Florida

Built on the assembly line and transported to the home site by truck, this comfortable and attractive two-bedroom, two-bath home, the *Ardmore*, is one of several models built by the Behring Corporation. Price for this 1,865-square-foot house, including a two-car garage, is $22,900. Framework is steel with interior walls of plaster and exterior walls of stucco. House has central air conditioning and heating, is completely carpeted and insulated. Kitchen and baths in all Behring homes have seamless vinyl floors and are completely equipped. All-electric kitchens include built-in ovens, food disposers, and dishwashers. Houses have full housepower wiring, TV outlets, and electric water heaters. Lots are fully sodded and driveways are paved. Screened porches or Florida rooms are available at extra cost. Behring communities are planned with green areas and recreational facilities. There are both adult retirement and family communities. Prices range from $14,990 to $26,490.

Floor Plan 1. Futura II, a two-bedroom, one-bath home that sells for $17,990. Price includes electric kitchen appliances and fenced courtyard. Carport optional. Central air conditioning and heating available at $995. Home is built on standard lot.

Floor Plan 2. The Branford, a three-bedroom, two-bath model with central air conditioning and heating and carport. Screened porch is available at an additional $1,900, garage at $795.

Floor Plan 1.

BEDROOM
11'1"x10'1"

CLOSET

BATH

STORAGE

UTIL | STOR

BEDROOM
11'1"x14'9"

CLO | CLOSET

KITCHEN

FENCED COURTYARD
INCLUDED

CAR PORT
(Optional)

LIVING ROOM
14'7"x15'0"

DINING ROOM
8'3"x7'6"

Floor Plan 2.

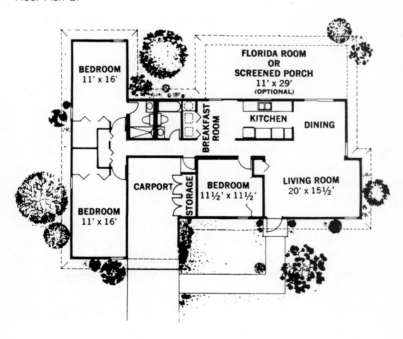

BEDROOM
11' x 16'

FLORIDA ROOM
OR
SCREENED PORCH
11' x 29'
(OPTIONAL)

BREAKFAST
ROOM

KITCHEN

DINING

CARPORT

STORAGE

BEDROOM
11½' x 11½'

LIVING ROOM
20' x 15½'

BEDROOM
11' x 16'

larger and more efficient outfits have jigs so that large quantities of lumber can be cut to the required length in one quick operation. Automatic nailing machines fasten the pieces together in a matter of seconds, and the work can continue regardless of the weather.

The time to order a panel house is in the late fall or winter, for this is the time in most areas when the weather is poor and a lot of outside construction stops. Then the men at the yard who don't have much to do are put to work turning out panels. If you get your order in during the bad weather, by the time you are ready to build, your house will have been partially completed right in the lumber yard.

This method of construction is very good if:

1. You are building in an area where the outside building season is relatively short.

2. You are building in an area where labor is scarce and there is an advantage in having as much preassembly work done as possible.

3. You want a custom-designed shell to complete yourself or to have completed when you can afford it.

PREFABS

Within the industry prefabs are usually referred to as "manufactured houses," or "panelized houses" but because that name applies to several types of houses, we'll call them by their old and most popular name: prefabs.

With the exception of modular houses, prefabs are the closest thing we have to a complete factory-built house. They are designed so that they can be built in panels or sections, and these are delivered to the site for assembly. Everything is included in the package—plumbing, wiring, heating, interior walls, trim, and kitchen equipment. The sections are complete right down to the paint so that when they are set in place and fastened together, the house is ready to be lived in.

Some years ago prefabs had a rather bad reputation. Even though their construction was often of a higher standard than that used by many conventional builders, the houses themselves were poorly designed and were more or less intended for the bottom of the economic home-buying market. Prefabs have changed their image a good deal since then, and some now have excellent designs and are of superior-quality materials and construction.

Prefabs are usually purchased through a local dealer or direct from the manufacturer. Usually the manufacturer or dealer assembles the house. Prices are for complete units with the exception of foundations, and the cost of the foundation will vary depending on soil conditions.

A prefab will run about $3.00 less per square foot than a conventional house and can usually be put up in a matter of weeks, as compared to the months it takes to build a standard house. Prefabs come in a wide range of prices starting at around $12,000 and going up to $50,000 or more. Many manufacturers have a special vacation-house line, but any of the smaller units can make a perfectly adequate leisure home. Unfortunately, prefabs are not allowed in every community because they come with the wiring and plumbing installed, and there are wide variations in building codes governing both these elements.

Prefabs are especially good if:

1. You want a house in a hurry.
2. You want to know in advance exactly what the house is going to cost.
3. You prefer to buy something ready-made rather than have to shop around and make a lot of decisions about design, type of heating system, brand and style of plumbing fixtures, type of construction, and so forth.

MODULAR HOUSES

Many authorities in the housing field believe that modular homes will be the housing of the future. A modular house combines some of the best features of the prefab and the mobile home, and many modulars are made by manufacturers of prefabs and mobile homes.

A modular house, which is sometimes called a sectional house, can be almost any size and style—a two-story house, attached units, even a multifamily dwelling. The house is so designed that it can be built in complete sections consisting of several rooms. The sections contain all the essential elements —wiring, plumbing, wall covering, and even paint. When the sections arrive at the site they can be quickly joined together to produce a complete structure. Modulars differ from prefabs primarily in that the completed units are far larger, and they differ from mobile homes in that they aren't restricted to any particular design or shape. The only restrictions on the size of the sections is that they be no wider or longer than can be shipped by truck, or a maximum of 14 feet wide and 64 feet long. But this is no great drawback because the manufacturers simply carve up any size house to meet these requirements. If the house requires a living room 28 feet wide, that section is cut in two to produce two units 14 feet wide.

The price advantage of modular houses over conventional ones is considerable. Savings can run from $2 to $5 a square foot depending on the design of the house and local building costs. This means that on a 1,200 square-foot house you would save between $2,400 and $6,000 on a modular over a stick-built.

Once the foundations are in, it takes only a few weeks to put up a large modular house, and a small one can often be completed in the matter of days. Like mobile homes, modulars are often available completely furnished.

Modular houses are especially good if:

1. You want a conventional house in a hurry.
2. You like the idea of buying a complete package, right down to the furnishings if you want.

3. You want to save considerable money over conventional construction.

MOBILE HOMES

These are about as complete "instant vacation housing" as you can find today. A mobile home, in case you don't know, isn't a trailer or a camper. It's a factory-built house that is equipped with wheels so it can be delivered to the home site. Once it is at the site it is placed on foundation piers and connected into the water and sewage system and into the electric and telephone lines.

Mobile homes come in all sizes up to 1,400 square feet, but the most popular are the 12-by-64-foot or 14-by-64-foot models. These provide a couple of bedrooms, a full bath, a large (or fairly large) living room, a good-size kitchen with a dining area either in the kitchen or off the living room. A unit of this kind starts at around $6,000 and goes up to around $8,000. Other units range in price from under $4,000 to over $18,000. Prices given on mobile homes include everything—kitchen appliances and basic furniture such as beds, dressers, tables, and lamps as well as draperies. If you are in the market for a low-cost vacation house, you should look into mobile homes. For the price, they're a whale of a bargain.

Of course, mobile homes are not perfect, and they don't make ideal vacation houses for everyone. First, they are not exactly what you might call spacious. Even the expandable units measure only about 24 to 28 feet wide with a maximum length of 64 feet, and this can be pretty close quarters for a family with a couple of active youngsters—or even a large dog. They are most popular among young couples with no children or perhaps only one child, or among older or retired people.

A major problem with mobile homes is that they aren't welcome everywhere. Many areas prohibit them even on the owner's own land, while others relegate them to mobile-home

communities or certain specified areas. Before you buy a mobile home, or a piece of land that you plan to put a mobile home
on, check with the zoning board or building authorities in the
area to see if you will be permitted to put a mobile home where
you intend to buy.

Many mobile-home owners put their units in mobile-home
communities or parks either because they prefer being part of
a community, don't own their own land, or find that this is the
only place where the community allows mobile homes. In a
mobile-home community you pay monthly rent for the site, and
this includes water and sewage. Electricity and telephone service is paid for by the individual homeowner. Rents vary from
$25 a month to over $100 depending on the community and the
services it supplies. Some of these communities are terrible—
you've probably seen a few along the side of the road that look
like a collection of metal shacks. But some are excellent. They
have good landscaping, large sites, and compare favorably
with a good community of conventional houses. Many communities are designed as resorts and have their own swimming
pools and other recreational facilities.

The better-quality mobile-home communities are not easy
to get into because space in them is much in demand. Many of
them are owned by mobile-home dealers, and the only way to
get space in the community is to buy a mobile home through
that particular dealer. If you want a mobile home in a good
mobile-home community, check the availability of sites before
you buy.

19
DOME HOUSES

Dome houses are a lot of fun. They are beginning to pop up all over the country not only as vacation houses but as year-round houses as well. Young people love them because they represent the *new* rather than yesterday. There is even an entire commune of dome houses in Colorado. But older people also like domes because they have much to offer besides their interesting shape. One of the things they offer is about the lowest cost per square foot that you can find today.

R. Buckminster Fuller originated the geodesic dome some twenty years ago. He saw it as a solution to low-cost housing because the geodesic dome covers a maximum area with a minimum of materials. The basic concept of the dome house is built around a system of triangular space frames that produce a self-reinforcing structure. The mathematics involved in the design and its execution are very complex. We don't even begin to understand them—but we do know that they work.

Domes can be built out of metal, clear plastic, opaque plastic, or wood. The most popular material appears to be wood—plywood with a waterproofing on the exterior side. The clear plastic domes are great if you want to know what's going on outside and aren't too concerned about privacy.

Domes are extremely versatile. They can be used as ski houses because they can withstand heavy snow loads, and they do well by the shore because they can also withstand strong winds. They can be used on every kind of a site depending on the floor system employed. On hillside construction, piers and a platform are used. On relatively even ground, wood or concrete slab floors are practical with or without a basement.

Because there are no interior bearing walls, the interior space of a dome house is very flexible and can be divided up to suit your needs. You can divide up the space with rigid partitions or you can keep it more open by using screens and curtains instead of partitions. And domes are easy to expand when more space is needed. It's just a matter of removing one of the exterior panels in the existing structure and sticking another dome alongside so the two can be connected. This makes a dome an ideal starter house. Domes can even be heated. The best method is with hot water or electric perimeter baseboard units.

A few daring souls have figured out the mathematics and built dome houses from their own designs. Some of these projects have been a success—some have not. The best and safest way to get a dome house of your own is to buy one from one of the several outfits that specialize in this kind of construction. What they offer is a precut or prefab house that is carefully engineered and delivered to the site in panels. It takes only a short time to set these panels together after the floor is in place. For example, a dome house with 1,700 square feet of living space, which includes a balcony, can be assembled by four men in about two days. Furthermore, no special tools or equipment of the kind often needed for other types of construction are called for. Putting up one of these manufactured domes is something you can often do yourself with the help of some friends.

At the present time, the manufactured domes cost from $10 to $12 a square foot complete. This is considerably less than you'll pay for conventional construction. Dome houses manufactured by reputable companies are so engineered that they

DOMES AND STOCK
PLAN HOUSES

The Dome House

Geodesic Structures, Inc.,
Hightstown, New Jersey

Photo 1. The dome house shown here is the 1,500-square-foot, 39-foot-diameter *D-39 Apollo,* consisting of living room, dining room, kitchen, bath, two bedrooms, and balcony. The system of triangular space frame, made of precision mill-beveled 2 x 4 kiln-dried Douglas fir frame members and exterior-grade plywood with a medium-density plastic overlay, creates a self-reinforcing roof and siding units based on the mathematically precise divisions of a sphere. These factory-assembled preinsulated frames are simply bolted together to form the finished building. The plywood is surface glued and stapled to the framing members. Different types of exterior finishes, such as the cedar shingles shown above, are optional.

Photos 2–6. This interesting sequence of how a dome is put together speaks for itself. Domes can be placed almost anywhere, depending on the floor system used. In 1972 Geodesic Structures was offering domes ranging in size and price from 485 square feet at $875 to 2,800 square feet at $12,950. The *D-39* being built here is 1,100 square feet and in 1972 was priced at $4,185 for the package. Four men can construct it in two days; smaller models take less time. No special tools or equipment are needed and complete assembly plans are supplied with each dome. Geodesic Structures ships anywhere in the United States with freight charges varying with model selected and point of destination.

3

4

5

6

Stock Plans
Southeastern Forest Experiment Station,
Forest Service,
U.S. Department of Agriculture

Photo 1. The house in the round shown here is one of several interesting designs of a program to develop new construction techniques that will lead to more efficient use of wood and wood products in low- and middle-income housing. Known as House Plan No. FS-SE-7, this three-bedroom, two bath home was built by designer Harold Zornig in Athens, Georgia, in 1970 for about $14,000, exclusive of land. It contains a lot of living space for the money and is novel without being impractical. Because none of the interior walls is load-bearing, the interior design can be worked out to suit individual needs.

The house is built on a circular concrete slab which is placed on concrete block (or brick) foundation wall with a treated lumber nailing strip fastened on the perimeter. Heating ducts may also be installed during the slab construction. The exterior walls consist of an inner and outer skin of 1-inch vertical tongue-and-groove boards, separated by 1-inch horizontal plywood bands, 2 feet apart, with insulation in the wall cavity. Walls are 4-foot-wide prefabricated modular panels. The Forestry Service suggests that 1-inch presawn softwood lumber with rough side exposed be used for both walls. The two layers of ½-inch thick plywood for the bands provides a 1-inch horizontal space in the wall for insulation and wiring. Doors and windows are cut into the walls after erection.

The roof system is composed of nail-laminated 5 by 6 radial beams nailed into slots in the inner and outer wall. Tongue-and-groove 1 by 6 decking is then installed and rigid foamed-in-place insulation applied directly to the exterior surface. This is then covered with a suitable roof covering to protect it from sunlight. The coated urethane is said to provide excellent waterproofed insulation without the need for conventional roofing.

Photo 2. View from family room into hall and living room shows circular center wall and beams and exposed roof decking. Radial plan is very pleasing to the eye. Partition walls are of a single-layer particle-board panels and fit into slots in roof beams. Frame partitions are used only in bathroom walls to conceal plumbing. Any conventional heating system can be installed.

Floor Plan. Round house of wood.

Photographs: Housing Research Unit, Forestry Sciences Laboratory, Athens, Ga.

1

Detailed plan and
specifications for this and other
designs are available without
charge from Housing Research,
Forestry Sciences Laboratory,
Carleton Street, Athens,
Georgia, 30601

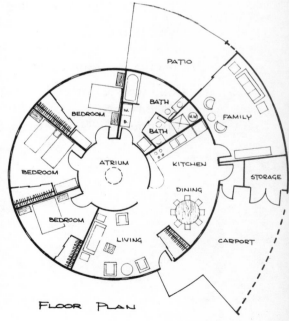

FLOOR PLAN

meet residential building codes. Nevertheless, before you buy a dome it would be wise to check with the local building authorities; there just might be some other restriction that prohibits them in your locality.

Here is a partial listing of firms manufacturing dome houses:

Geodesic Structures, Inc.
9 West Union Avenue
Bound Brook, New Jersey 08805

Cadco Corp.
Box 874
Plattsburgh, New York 12901

Cathedralite
P.O. Box B
Daly City, California 94000

Dome East
325 Duffy Avenue
Hicksville, New York 11800

Dyna Dome Co.
22226 North 23 Avenue
Phoenix, Arizona 85000

Domeworks, Corp.
P.O. Box 712
Albuquerque, New Mexico 87100

STOCK
PLANS

If you want a more or less professionally designed vacation house without having to go to the expense of hiring an architect, consider the advantages of using stock plans. Many firms specialize in this field, and they offer catalogues in ads found in shelter, outdoor, and women's magazines as well as on newsstands. Several of the large lumber manufacturers' associations offer plans, and so do some local newspapers. Builders who specialize in vacation houses usually have a supply of stock plans around to help their clients decide what they want, and so do large lumber yards and building-supply outfits.

There is considerable variation in the quality of design in these plans. Some were originally done by talented architects and designers, but the vast majority are ground out by draftsmen who produce endless variations on the same theme. The price of stock plans also varies. Some plans cost only $5 or $10 and may provide minimum information. Others cost $50 to $100 and give very complete plans as well as a list of specifications and materials. In some cases you can order an inexpensive plan that gives a general overview on the basis of which you then decide whether you want to spend considerably more money for the more detailed plan.

177

A particular set of stock plans is usually ordered on the basis of what you have seen and liked in the price list or catalogue. Usually both floor plans and exterior renderings are shown. Now you can believe what you see in a floor plan, but don't rely on a rendering of the exterior of the house. In many cases, a two-color or black-and-white rendering of a house has little relationship to what it will look like after it is finished. A fair-to-middling artist can take the floor plan of a boxcar and turn out a rendering that will look like an architectural gem. He can take a little nothing of a house and stretch it out to make it look like your true dream home. He'll soften up the lines, give it beautiful proportions, and then, just to clinch the deal, add a dozen old trees or palms around the front, a nice floating dock off the east terrace, and miles and miles of spacious decks. Don't ever believe renderings unless they are done by your own architect. If you want to know what the house will look like after it's built, wait until you've got the plans and then look at the front and rear elevations. These will show you what you're going to get.

Vast numbers of stock plans are sold each year but relatively few of the houses ever get built. One reason for this is that when a family takes the plans to a builder to get a bid on construction, they find that the house is far too expensive for them. Yet it is easy enough to know about what it will cost to build a house before you go ahead and order an expensive set of plans. Most offerings for stock plans state the number of square feet the house contains. All you have to do is to multiply this figure by the square-foot cost of construction. If it's a simple summer house, multiply by $15; if it's a year-round vacation house, multiply the total square feet by $25. In other words, if the house contains 1,500 square feet and it's a simple summer place, it will cost around $22,500—not including land. If it's a year-round place it will cost $37,500—not including land.

Stock plans can be especially good when you aren't sure exactly what you want. You can go through a catalogue until you see something that looks close to what you are after and, when the plans arrive, start fooling with them to make the house better for your particular needs. Anyway, this is what many people who build with stock plans have done. It's wise if you do your fooling around on tissue paper placed over the floor plan. When you get something you think is right for you, draw the changes in lightly on the plan and then discuss them with your builder. You need to know if your changes are practical before going too far with them.

Stock plans of small houses are good for the do-it-yourselfer. Besides providing a far more detailed set of blueprints than you could draw yourself, they also include a materials list so you'll know what you need. And if you take this materials list to a lumber yard, they can give you a figure on what the materials will cost.

21 CONDOMINIUMS

The term *condominium* does not refer to a particular kind of house but rather to a type of ownership: a condominium is a multiunit dwelling in which the individuals own their own units (or apartments) outright and share with other owners joint ownership of all common property. The joint holdings include the land on which the condominium is built, the halls and lobby, elevators, and all common facilities such as landscaping, parking areas, and recreational facilities that are part of the complex.

The operation and maintenance of all the jointly held property is in the hands of a management group which in turn is under the supervision of a group of owners elected by all the owners of units in the condominium. The management group is supported by a maintenance charge levied against each owner of a dwelling unit.

A condominium has a great many advantages over buying a co-op or simply renting a vacation house. Because you legally own your unit or apartment under this arrangement, you have the same advantages as if you owned your own home. You can finance the purchase through a conventional mortgage loan exactly as you would a house. With each payment you make, you increase your equity in your home so that when the loan has been paid off, you own your home free and clear. You can deduct the interest on the mortgage on your income tax. You can sell your unit, remodel it, and do exactly what you want with it.

Condominiums have become very popular in the vacation-house field for many good reasons. First, they provide most of the advantages of owning your own house without the responsibilities and many of the headaches associated with home-ownership—especially vacation-home ownership. In a condominium you don't have to worry about outside maintenance and repairs. You have no lawns to cut, siding to paint, or septic systems to worry about. It's up to the management to take care of such chores and to worry about the heating and plumbing systems and about getting the snow off the driveways and parking areas. All you are concerned about is the interior of your particular unit, and if you don't ever want to redecorate the walls or refinish the floors, that's your business. All this leaves you with a good deal of time to use as you wish. Many of the more expensive vacation condominiums provide all sorts of additional services—at a price, of course. They can handle all your housework, prepare your meals, and furnish you with a baby sitter.

Another great advantage of condominiums is that they can offer a great range in the size of the dwellings. For example, many have studio units that are quite adequate for a single person or a couple, especially if they just want to use the unit on weekends. Other units contain one bedroom, while much larger units are also available in the same condominium. If a family can make do in relatively small quarters, they can buy a condominium unit in an area with facilities they could never afford if they went out to buy or build a comfortable house in the same region.

Equally important is the fact that a condominium can provide a better environment for vacation living than would be possible for most families in a single-family house. For example, oceanfront property is so expensive today that it is no longer economically feasible for an individual to buy a lot and put up a house. But if that same size lot is utilized for a multilevel condominium, the cost of the land can be divided among many dwellings and consequently, for what would be the fraction of the cost of the land alone, a family can have an oceanside home in the condominium. This same advantage holds true no matter where the condominium is built, and it also applies to man-made recreational facilities that may be a part of the complex—swimming pools, golf courses, and tennis courts. As the construction and maintenance of these facilities are spread among many families, the cost to each is relatively low.

Many ecologists and conservationists favor the condominium approach because it utilizes land more efficiently and with more regard to our diminishing land resources than does single-family housing. Single-family houses waste vast amounts of land with much of it going for nothing more than to ensure privacy between dwellings. With condominiums, the dwelling units are concentrated in one area and the unused portion of the land can be set aside for common recreational use or even as wilderness and wildlife preserves. Also, because they are multifamily units, there are more local and state regulations on how condominiums can be built, and this means not only better planning but also underground utilities, central sewer systems, and so forth.

There are two basic types of condominiums. Type A is made up of attached dwellings, and these consist of more or less individual one- or two-story houses set together in about the same fashion as the new "town house" developments or the older row houses or brownstones. Living in one of these is much the same as living in a conventional single-family house except that you are physically joined to the house (or houses) adjacent to yours. Type B is the high-rise or multilevel condominium, which is much the same as a high-rise apartment.

Condominiums are not perfect for every family or individual either as year-round or vacation houses. They have some obvious drawbacks. One of the most important of these is that while you do *own* your unit, you only *share* in the ownership of the common property. How common property is to be maintained or improved is up to the majority of the owners. They may elect to cut down on certain services to avoid an increase in maintenance charges or they may vote to increase services not essential to you. In the latter case, this would mean higher maintenance charges for something you don't want.

You are also not going to be able to avoid coming into contact with some of the other owners, and this is especially true of a vacation setup where recreational facilities such as a swimming pool are often part of the complex. If you find none of the people to your liking, it may dampen your pleasure somewhat. But it is also possible to live around people and still maintain your privacy—many apartment dwellers have lived in the same building for years and have only a nodding acquaintance with their next-door neighbors.

Condominiums aren't much fun for the gardener unless you get one of those units that includes a back yard. They are also not much fun for the do-it-yourselfer.

Condominiums come in all price ranges. What you pay depends not only on the size of your unit but also on the location of the condominium and the amount of recreational services it provides. For $20,000 or so you can pick up a studio apartment in a recreational area, but when you start looking in the same area for enough space for a family you are talking about $30,000 or more.

There are quite a few things to check into when you begin looking at condominiums. Aside from the basic price, you will want to find out what the maintenance is going to cost—and you should keep in mind that it is probably going to increase over the years just like everything else. If you use a mortgage loan to make the purchase, the mortgage payments will remain the same. The maintenance will not. The maintenance charge is also going to go up if there are unfinished facilities to be completed. If a swimming pool is projected for the future, for example, you can bet your bottom dollar it's going to add to your costs when it gets into operation.

You also want to take a look at the kind of people you are going to have as close neighbors. As we said before, you don't have to socialize with your neighbors, but it will certainly help if you are more or less on the same wavelength. We once spent a few days at a very fancy condominium leisure apartment where drinking began around the pool at eleven in the morning and went on until the pool closed up at midnight. It was really a hard-drinking crowd and it took us a week to recover from the experience.

If you have small children, look for a condominium that has or will attract familes with children. Some condominiums make an effort to have families with children and provide special recreational facilities for the kids. But other condominiums don't like kids and this can be pretty dull for the young.

Check over all the regulations concerning the operation of the condominium yourself, but also have an attorney explore the entire operation before you buy. As in the case of a planned vacation development, you want to make as certain as you can that promises will be kept.

22

HOUSEBOATS

For certain families, a houseboat can make an ideal weekend and vacation place. And they have several advantages over a house. They don't need an expensive piece of land and costly improvements—a well, septic system, roads, landscaping, and utilities. There is no real estate tax to pay, and you don't have to worry about community affairs or the neighborhood. If you don't like neighbors, get tired of the same view, or want better swimming or fishing, you just have to turn on the engine, pull up the anchor, and take off. If you enjoy swimming, water sports, fishing, or just relaxing, all your recreational facilities are right around you.

There are also some disadvantages. First and foremost, living for an extended period on even a large houseboat is somewhat confining to some people. Then you'll need liability insurance for your houseboat so that if you smash up the dock or somebody else's boat, you will be covered. This can cost around $400 a year. You will also have to pay for docking and this can run as much as $800 for a summer season. More and more states are passing antipollution laws that require houseboats to have waste-holding tanks for raw sewage, and an adequate tank can be an expensive addition to a boat. You also have to

185

go to a marina and pay to have the tank pumped out at frequent intervals. And while the hull of the boat may not require much maintenance, the engines will and you'll also have to supply them with gasoline or diesel oil.

Today's houseboats have been described as floating mobile homes, which is a pretty apt description. Aside from the fact that many of them look like floating mobile homes, they contain many of the same comforts and conveniences. There is a well-equipped galley (kitchen), a head (bathroom) complete with a shower and hot water, bedrooms, a living room, and even heat and air conditioning. Houseboats come equipped with built-in furniture and carpets, and the interior space is as efficiently arranged as you find in a mobile home. The hulls of fiber glass, aluminum, or reinforced concrete require a minimum amount of maintenance and the same holds true of the decks and superstructure. And, like mobile homes, a lot of people are against them—especially owners of waterfront houses who object to a lot of houseboats sitting offshore spoiling the view and often dumping trash and garbage overboard to spoil the swimming and litter the shorefront.

Houseboats range in price from around $5,000 to over $100,000, with the most popular types falling into the $10,000-to-$15,000 range. For this sort of money you can get a houseboat that sleeps four people with all the essentials for living, but it's going to be tight, especially in bad weather when the sun deck can't be used. It is only when you move up into the $20,000 range or higher that you get what we consider to be comfortable interior space for the average family. Even so, the typical houseboat is far more comfortable for living than the same-size cabin cruiser. The living area, bedrooms, and kitchen are all topside so there is better light and better ventilation than you'll find in all but the largest cabin cruisers.

Houseboats require less experience and skill to operate than cabin cruisers. One reason for this is that houseboats don't go as fast and another is that they are generally confined to quiet waters—rivers, lakes, or inland waterways. Only the very large houseboats are suitable for off-shore cruising.

Most people familiar with houseboats agree that before you buy it is wise to rent a boat for a weekend or so to see how it goes. This is especially important if you have never spent much time on the water or in a small craft. You can rent a houseboat for around $400 a week. The dealer will check you out in the operation of the boat so you'll more or less know what you are doing. Speaking of renting, there seems to be a good market for houseboat rentals. Some families rent their boat out at certain times to help defray costs. Some dealers will handle all these arrangements for you.

Houseboats seem to appeal primarily to families who have grown children or children old enough to take care of themselves in and about the water. A houseboat is not ideal if you have small children who require constant supervision. If they can't play in the water about all they can do on the boat is watch TV or get in your hair.

Houseboats seem to be most popular on fresh water—lakes, rivers and delta country—places where the waters are relatively quiet. They are not as popular on salt water because it can be rough at times even in sheltered areas, and while the hull designs of houseboats are extremely stable, a good squall can shake you up a bit and certainly make it difficult to play gin rummy or get a good night's sleep.

What size and type of houseboat to buy depends on when and where you plan to use it. Some families use their boats only for day trips, so that speed is more important than sleeping and cooking facilities. Some keep them tied up at a dock or anchored for the entire season, and therefore speed and seaworthiness are not as important as living space. We know one family that owns a large houseboat on a very muddy artificial lake in the Southwest. They just use it as a place to get a cool night's sleep becase they don't like air conditioning.

How a houseboat is used depends somewhat on your age. Younger families are more apt to use a houseboat to explore whereas older couples are more inclined to park the boat someplace and relax. If you live near a body of water that is worth exploring, you'll want a houseboat with a shallow draft so you can move away from channels. The twin-hull catamarans or flat-bottomed hulls are better for this than the more maneuverable V-hulls.

Before you get too involved in the idea of owning a houseboat, find out where you can use it. They are not allowed everywhere. And also find out what it is going to cost you to dock it. Also, like everything else in the vacation-house field, houseboats are offered with a lot of optional features. When you find one you like, be sure to check with the dealer to see exactly what is included in the basic price and what those optional features are going to cost.

23

PLANNED
VACATION
COMMUNITIES

There is a relatively new breed of cat springing up all over the country called a "planned vacation community" or "planned vacation development." You might say its lineage is equal parts conventional residential housing development, summer and winter resort, and country club. The emphasis is on fun along with comfort and convenience.

Don't confuse a planned vacation community with one of those typical recreational land sales outfits. These concerns have been around for years. All they do is find a big chunk of inexpensive land somewhere, divide it up into home sites, and sell the sites. In many cases the nearest recreational facilities are many miles away and consist of a public beach or state park. The "nearby year-round playground" mentioned in the advertisement for one of these outfits turned out to be the Rocky Mountains.

In the communities we are talking about you can expect to find within the community and for the more or less exclusive use of its members such facilities as a golf course, tennis courts, swimming pool, boating and fishing, bridle paths, saunas, shuffleboard courts, and a clubhouse or recreational center. In

189

the colder climates there will also be facilities for skiing, snow-mobiling, ice skating, and even ice boating.

You will find these communities by the ocean, in the mountains, in the desert—anyplace where there are natural recreational facilities or where the climate and terrain allow for man-made facilities. You will also find developers who have, literally, bought an entire rundown village, reconstructed it, and then built their vacation community around it.

Some vacation communities are designed exclusively for single-family houses, and others provide attached or high-rise condominium units. The primary emphasis in some communities is on vacation and leisure living; in others the approach is more to provide year-round living or retirement homes. In some it is hard to find anyone in residence who is under fifty, and children are as scarce as hen's teeth; others are designed to appeal to younger families with small children. And there are also those communities that are after the young set—the swingers.

There are many reasons for the growth and popularity of these communities. One big reason is the demand for more and more varied recreational facilities. Just providing a lake or an ocean to swim in isn't enough anymore. People want a golf course, a heated swimming pool so they can take a dip after skiing, and all the rest of those playthings. And more playthings keep becoming popular. Who would have thought five or ten years ago that there would be a crying need for snowmobile trails?

People want more creature comforts. They like the convenience of a clubhouse where they can entertain without having to cook or wash dishes, and where someone else worries when something goes wrong with the plumbing, or sees to it that the roads and driveways get plowed and the community is protected from intruders. It is also a fact that it's getting hard to find a small parcel of land in a good recreational area, and when you do it costs like blazes to buy and improve it. Even today's growing concern about conservation and ecology have helped stimulate the growth of planned communities, for often they are the only practical means of utilizing the land without doing it great ecological harm. For there can be little doubt that a planned vacation community that has been put together with the professional guidance of land planners, architects, engineers, landscape designers, and ecologists is a far better way to use our remaining land than the haphazard approach of the past. You merely have to visit some of the older vacation communities to see how poorly we have used some of our best natural recreation land. Drive along ocean and lake shores that were developed a few years ago and what do you find? Mile after mile of tacky little cottages, one on top of the other, each one set on a tiny strip of waterfront property so that the view as well as access to the water is denied to everyone else. We once drove three miles along a beach road on the New England coast and only twice was there a hole in the solid wall of houses that allowed you to see the ocean only a hundred or so yards from the road.

A well-planned vacation community can eliminate many of the horrors that have become a part of our older vacation areas. The planners can develop the land so that a natural facility such as a lake or shoreline is available to all members of the community rather than only to those who can afford to buy the expensive waterfront lots. They can set aside certain tracts of land as greenbelts and for common use, and control the design and type of houses that can be built. And they can protect the ecology of the area. It helps, of course, if local and state laws require the developer to do all these things rather than leaving the matter completely in his hands.

Planned vacation communities are big business. Some of them are underwritten by huge corporations, for they often require the outlay of millions of dollars simply to get started. Last summer we visited one community that was just getting underway. The project involved around 3,000 acres of woodland and included a lake about one and a half miles long. Every inch of the land had been meticulously surveyed and engineered to comply with state and local laws. The developers knew almost as much about that particular parcel of land as the Creator and Mother Nature combined.

Certain areas had been set aside for roads, others for home sites, recreational areas, and as wilderness for the comfort and convenience of wild animals, birds, and nature lovers. Houses were to be grouped in clusters and served by a central sewage system to eliminate the need for individual septic systems. Utility lines were to be set underground, lawns were to be forbidden so that there would be no noise pollution from power mowers, and members of the community could not use outboard motors on the lake. And, naturally, there would be all sorts of recreational facilities—enough to leave you completely exhausted at the end of the day.

Not all communities are planned this carefully or on such a grand scale. Some are small—a few hundred acres—but excellent all the same. Some are small and very poor. And some of the very large ones have turned out to be disastrous for the land as well as the home buyer. Some communities start off with a big promotion bang and never reach the final state of completion. And in spite of a lot of federal, state, and local laws, there is always a chance of getting a bum deal if you don't watch your step. But if a vacation community provides what you are looking for, and you take the time to find a good one, you'll be happy.

HOW DO THEY WORK?

Basically, the idea goes like this. When you buy a building site in the community or build a house there, you become a member of the owners' association, or whatever it is called, and this gives you the right to use the common facilities such as golf course, swimming pool, clubhouse, and so forth. There is usually some sort of yearly charge involved for the use of the facilities as well as one for maintenance of the community.

The community is run by a management group. It operates and maintains all the common areas and facilities and also sees that the various codes, covenants, and restrictions are enforced. At the start, the management group is set up by the developer. This arrangement may continue if the developer sticks with the community after it has been completed, but if he moves out, the management group will be under the supervision of a group of property owners elected by all members of the community.

Some developers of these vacation communities are interested only in selling land, and it is up to the buyer of a home site to get a house built that meets the requirements of the community. Other developers sell both houses and land and you either buy their houses or none. In between, there are all sorts of different arrangements. Some developers have a design group who will plan a house for the owner of a home site and arrange to have it built by a construction firm; others have several builders you can choose from.

HOW MUCH DO THEY COST?

You've got two considerations here: the price of land and the price of the house—and the combination is going to vary depending on the kind and size of site you select and the community. In a rather typical community an average building site may run from $5,000 to $10,000, but if you want a more desirable site, such as one on the waterfront or golf course, the price may be $20,000 or more. And in a good community, the cost of the house is going to be high. There will be regulations as to size and quality of the house. You won't, for example, be able to put up a little summer cabin or have a mobile home or perhaps even a log cabin. What you are probably talking about in most communities is a house that will cost from $25,000 up, plus land.

HOW DO YOU FIND THEM?

This isn't too difficult. Many of the large out-of-state as well as local developments advertise in local newspapers. The very big ones advertise in national magazines—especially the home and recreational publications. You can also get a list of communities by writing to the Department of Development or Recreation in your particular state or to the state's chamber of commerce. Most of these communities have their own sales force so they aren't usually listed through local real estate brokers.

Once you've answered a few advertisements or written away for literature, you can expect a lot of action. You may, for example, receive a phone call from a developer asking when a representative can drop around to your house to talk with you about the wonders of their community. The representative will show up, if you want, complete with a movie projector, and you'll get a good hard sales pitch. Or, you may be invited to come and spend the night (at the developer's expense) so you can get a firsthand impression of what's going on. Lots of outfits will invite you and other interested families in your area to a dinner at some local spot so they can show you a film and give you a sales talk.

This kind of aggressive selling is not limited to fly-by-night outfits or those in less desirable communities. Some of the best and largest developers use these same methods. So don't be turned off from a community simply because they twist your arm a bit. And don't turn down an offer to visit the place at the developer's expense if you are really interested. You certainly don't want to buy something unless you've had a chance to inspect it firsthand, and if the developer is willing to pay your way, you might as well let him. But don't sign *anything* until you have really checked out the community, and don't feel obligated to buy because the developer gave you a free meal or put you up for the night at a motel—which he probably owns.

Some of the communities you visit or read about will be fairly well established. A good number of sites will have been sold and houses built on them. The recreational facilities will be complete, and a visual inspection can give you a fair idea of what the place is like and what sort of people you will have as neighbors. But many communities are not this far along. You may find, as we did on numerous occasions, that with the exception of the sales office, the project is pretty much still a plan or projection. Regardless of what shape the community is in, you've got to check it out carefully if you don't want to get burned.

BEFORE YOU BUY

When you buy into a vacation community, you not only buy a parcel of land and a house, you also buy a lot of promises. If it is an established community that is more or less completed, you buy the promise that what you find and like will continue, not only for your own enjoyment but also to protect your investment. If you are buying into a community that is just getting started, you buy the promise that all the facilities planned for will come about in the immediate future. Sometimes all these promises don't come true. When they don't, it may be the fault of the developer, it may be an act of God, or it may be that they were the kind of promises that should never have been made in the first place—or accepted by you—because they were beyond anyone's control.

What you want to make sure of before you buy is that all or most of the promises will come true. You can do a lot of investigating on your own, but you are going to need an attorney to do some of it for you. Here are some of the points you can check out on your own:

What does the community offer in the way of recreational facilities? Are these the facilities you and your family require?

How much is it all going to cost? This includes the price of the land, the cost of building or buying a house to meet the community as well as your requirements, and the yearly amount you'll have to pay for maintenance and service.

The reputation of the developer. This is essential regardless of whether it is an established community or one just getting started. Find out if he has done other communities, where they are located, and if possible visit them to see what they are like. Find out from the developer who is financing the project. Large, reputable corporations look at this type of project as a long-term investment, but a group of unknowns may be in it just as a speculative venture, and if they make a killing, some of it may come out of your hide. Find out if there is any local financing; local banks and investment houses usually don't get into anything that might hurt their local image.

Who are the people who are working on the project? Get their names and backgrouds. This list would include the land planners, engineers, architects, designers, and so forth. If this group is made up of recognized professionals in their fields it is a good sign, but if they are unknowns—often friends or relatives of the developer, with no previous experience in this type of project—you had better stay clear of it.

How good is the master plan of the community? Note how much land has been set aside for recreational facilities and common use and how much is devoted to building sites. Obviously you'll find that in the better communities a larger percentage of land is devoted to common use than in the sleazy developments where every inch of land is used for profitable building sites. But you will also find that in some communities land set aside for common use is useless for building sites or anything else. The developer who sets aside swamps, ravines, and cliffs as common land isn't doing anyone a favor. Ask the salesman to show you the land for common use.

Check the location and size of the building sites. If there is a body of water on the property, check to see if the developer has put building sites along the waterfront or if he has set the sites away from the shoreline so that the view and use of the water can be enjoyed by all members of the community regardless of the location of their particular home site. Also check the size of the building sites. In a well-designed community there will be large sites of an acre or more as well as small lots, but in the less desirable communities you'll find just a lot of minimum-size lots.

What sort of lots are available in your price range? In much of the sales literature, the building site pictured is the most expensive one while the price indicated is for the least expensive site. Drive around with a salesman and look at the actual sites in your price range.

What sort of people are you going to have as neighbors? This is very important. In a community of this type you are obviously going to be more in contact with other members of the community than you would if you were building on your own lot someplace. Don't tell the salesman what kind of people you like because he'll say that he community is getting this very type. Try to get him to offer information on the people buying into the community. Toss him a little bait by saying, "We visited one community and it was simply crawling with small children." By the time the salesman has finished you'll probably know if most of the buyers in this community are older people with grown children, don't have children, or don't like children.

What utilities does the developer provide? This would include water and sewage along with electricity and telephone.

Financing? Find out if the developer can provide financing and also what sort of terms he gives. Also check with local lending institutions to see what terms they can offer you.

While you can check out a good many aspects of a community by looking around and asking questions, many other important points can be answered only by someone with legal training. We suggest you use a local attorney to check out the following points.

Has the development been approved by all agencies involved? This would include federal regulations regarding land sales as well as state and local regulations covering land development and use.

Will the community be completed as planned and be maintained? This would include checking to find out if the developer has posted a performance bond or made some other legal arrangement to ensure that all the facilities promised will be provided within a reasonable length of time. It would also include examining convenants and restrictions and the arrangements made by the management (and future managements) to enforce these restrictions.

Can you get clear title to the land you buy? And if so, when? Unless you can get a warranty deed you should not buy the land. And you should get such a deed when you make your initial payment.

What about roads? It's important to find out the roads that must be maintained by the community and those that will be acceptable as town roads and therefore be maintained by the local township.

A planned vacation community is a highly complex concept by its very nature. Take your time to check most carefully the one you are interested in.

COMMUNITY LIVING

Condominiums
Unihab/Sugarbush and Drumleys, Warren, Vermont

The condominium concept of multifamily dwellings, either as attached houses or high-rise apartments, is gaining rapidly in popularity not only as primary housing but also for vacation and leisure homes. By grouping living units around common grounds and jointly owned open spaces, more people can have the advantages of living amid magnificient natural surroundings at less cost to themselves and at less expense to the ecology. The leisure-home condominium can save you a lot of the headaches that usually go along with home ownership—somebody else, usually a management company, sees that the grass is mowed, the snow plowed, and the recreational facilities kept in top shape.

The two condominiums shown, Unihab/Sugarbush and Drumleys, both in the Green Mountain National Forest area of Vermont, are especially attractive examples of this leisure-home concept. Unihab, dramatically contemporary in architecture, has spectacular views of the Sugarbush ski area and of Sugarbush Valley, and is convenient to ski lifts, stores, and restaurants. Drumleys is in the Mad River Valley, between Sugarbush Valley and the Glen Ellen and Mad River Glen ski areas. Both are established communities with plans for future expansion.

Photo 1. Unihab/Sugarbush, distinctive modular living units designed by architect Art Klipfel of Cambridge, Massachusetts, are engineered for flexibility of design, privacy, and the conveniences of modern condominium living. A total of eighty units is eventually planned for this complex. Prices have ranged from $15,000 for the two-bedroom units to $30,500 for a four-bedroom unit, but the newer units may be higher. Although built in clusters, all units are planned for private enjoyment with either individual balconies or terraces. Special attention has been given to the development of roadways, walkways, and paths that lead to an adjacent ski trail and to the village. Exterior walls consist of ⅝-inch Texture 1–11 plywood glued and nailed to the house framework. Surface is treated with stain. Floor and roof surfaces are insulated with 6-inch-thick insulation, walls, with 3⅝-inch insulation. Heating is electric with individual room thermostats. Kitchen appliances include a dishwasher, disposal unit, range, and refrigerator. Floors are carpeted throughout and interior lighting is recessed. Fireplaces and furnishings are optional.

Unihab Site Plan.

Photo 2. Drumley's Project, Phase 2, will add twenty-four units to the original ten. Designed by architect Robert Burley of Waitsfield, Vermont, the units are based on a "country house" concept to form a cluster community geared to year-round living. The natural properties of the site are retained by building the houses on the thickly wooded ridges while leaving the meadowland as a central common area. Recreational facilities consist of a swimming pool, golf course, tennis courts, numerous ski areas, and canoeing. A long-range planting program is in progress to achieve privacy, screening for parking, and attractive landscaping. A covered parking area gives direct access to the main entrance and a bedroom with bath on the lower level are accessible from inside or outside the house so that the space can be rented, if desired. Exterior front and rear walls of living, dining and kitchen level are of glass to capture the scenic outdoors and add a feeling of spaciousness. Bedroom level with bath is directly accessible from main living area as well as a sleeping loft or storage area. Four units have living room, dining room, and kitchen on the second level, with bedrooms above. The other units have these areas on a third level, with bedrooms on the second level.

Exposed beams inside the houses support a simple floor and roof-decking system, allowing maximum glass areas at each end of the units. Prices range from $39,000 to $42,500 complete.

Photograph: Dennis Curran

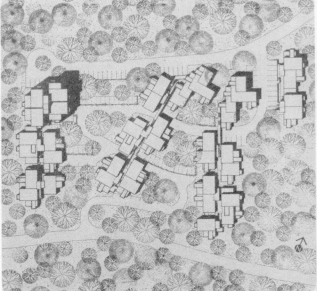

2

The Planned
Vacation Community
Gold Key Lake, Milford, Pennsylvania

Judging by the number of vacation-community developments now in existence and being planned, vacation-home ownership on one's own plot of ground but in a community setting is attracting a great many people. Fairly typical is the Gold Key Lake development in the Pocono Mountains. Planned around a 20-acre natural spring-fed lake, lots here are subdivided into 1/3-acre plots ranging in price from $5,000 to $35,000. The development is intended for those who enjoy community living and sports amid like-minded people. Gold Key offers plenty to do—boating, swimming, fishing, tennis courts, a putting green, and several good golf courses within easy driving distance. They have planned activities such as picnics, hayrides, and outdoor art shows. Winter brings ice skating, ice fishing, tobogganing, and regulated snowmobiling. There are several good ski spots in the general area and an all-year community lodge where dances and other social functions are held, in addition to providing overnight accommodations for guests. This community has its own volunteer fire department, a security adviser, a private road-maintenance crew, a Home and Property Owner's Association, and a quarterly intracommunity newspaper. Further development and improvements are continuing.

If not overdeveloped and if proper regard is paid to the environment and the safeguarding of natural resources, such communities can be rewarding and pleasant refuges for many people.

Photo 1. In order to avoid a "development" look, at Gold Key Lake the corporation limits the number of houses that can be built from a single model. But sufficient new designs are continually coming in so that prospective homeowners have plenty of choice. *The Foxwood,* the three-bedroom, two-bath house shown here, is a Leisure Homes, Inc. prefab with a base price about $29,000. Specifications include digging and backfilling the foundation and clearing the land 10 feet around the house. Siding is redwood and the house has electric heat and full insulation, plus storm windows and screens throughout. Hardwood floors are included in the price as are complete baths, kitchen cabinets, range, and 12-cubic-foot refrigerator. Houses have built-in vacuum systems.

Floor Plan. Double sliding-glass doors open onto upper and lower sun decks. Large family room on lower level can be used as such, or converted into additional sleeping area.

Photo 2. This one-story 24-by-36 house with insulated-glass gable-front wall is custom built on site by the Milford Resort Construction Co. Base price of around $17,600 includes poured-concrete footing, masonry-block foundation walls, plus excavation. Exterior walls are Texture 1-11. The house has electric heat and is completely wired and fully insulated. Price includes kitchen appliances and cabinets, driveway, and wraparound deck.

1

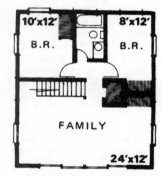

FIRST FLOOR

10'x12'
B.R.

8'x12'
B.R.

FAMILY

24'x12'

2

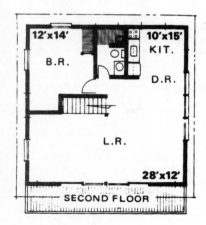

SECOND FLOOR

12'x14'
B.R.

10'x15'
KIT.

D.R.

L.R.

28'x12'

24

MODEL HOUSES

The model house is a familiar structure in the vacation-house field even as it is in the year-round-house field. Developers of vacation communities as well as manufacturers and dealers in prefabs, modular, panelized, shell, and mobile homes have found that the best way to sell their houses is to put up a model so that prospective customers can see what the finished product looks like and what a fine value it is for the money. Advertisements and brochures can get people interested, but before most people are willing to fork over money, they want to see exactly what the money is going to buy.

You'll find these model or "show" houses along the side of the road, in vacation developments, or on the grounds of manufacturers and dealers who have vacation dwellings to sell. You can learn a lot by visiting a model house. In fact, we urge you to visit a model or existing house before you buy anything in the field. There is nothing like a firsthand look. But you've got to know the rules of the game: what to look for, what to discount, and what questions to ask.

First, keep in mind that the seller has done just about everything he can think of to make the model look great—even greater than it is. The grounds around it will be beautifully

landscaped and perfectly maintained. There may be some extra touches such as window boxes loaded with lovely flowers,
a rustic fence, and maybe a few reproductions of old street
lamps. When you step inside, you will find the house completely furnished and decorated. The furnishings won't always
be to your taste, but even so they give the house a lived-in look.
If you look more carefully you may notice that the furniture is
not full size but slightly scaled down so that the rooms appear
larger than they actually are. There will be expensive draperies around the windows, thick carpeting on the floor, expensive
wallpaper on some of the walls. You may even notice a few
antiques. The kitchen will be a showcase of labor-saving appliances, and if it happens to be a warm day the air conditioning
will be keeping the inside of the house pleasantly cool. When
you look again at the price of the house, it all seems too good
to be true.

Well, it is. The price is for the house; it doesn't include all
that fancy landscaping and it doesn't include the furnishings,
draperies, carpeting, or wallpaper. For the price quoted, you
will get the sink, cabinets, and maybe the kitchen range, but
everything else is going to cost extra—including the air conditioning.

The first thing you will want to know, therefore, is exactly
what the basic price of the house includes. Some model homes
have a listing in each room that states which items are included in the base price and which are optional and their cost.
More often you will have to ask the salesman. He'll tell you, but
to get the complete picture you may have to ask about each
specific item in question.

If you are still interested after you get this information,
start checking the place out. Go into each room and try to picture it without its present furnishings. What would *you* be
putting into it? It's best if the entire family visits the house at
the same time. Some outfits don't allow children inside a model
house, but if children are allowed, bring them in. A room with
two people in it may seem perfectly comfortable, but when four
or five are in the family, and everyone is in the same room at

the same time—as would be the case with the living room or kitchen—things can get pretty crowded.

On most models it's hard to check out construction and workmanship because, naturally, if there were areas where workmanship or materials were not up to par, they would have been replaced. On the other hand, if you find poor workmanship in the model, you can bet your last dollar that it will turn up to a greater degree in any house put up by the same concern. Ask for basic information on materials used for walls, floors, siding, and roof. Find out if the house comes insulated, if the sliding glass doors are made of insulating glass, and the type and brand of plumbing and kitchen fixtures used.

And don't visit only the models in one development or from one particular manfacturer. Visit as many models in your area as you can. Pick up as much literature on each one as is available. Make notes on the additional information you get on each one from the salesman or through your own observation. When you have time, study all the information with care. You can compare the cost of space offered in each model by dividing the number of square feet of living space into the price of the house. For example, if a house contains 1,105 square feet of living space and sells for $23,205 the cost per square foot will be $21.00. This will give you the cost per square foot, and obviously the house that offers the lowest cost per square foot is the best from one point of view. But don't forget to take other considerations into account as well: the design of the exterior, the layout of the rooms, the quality of materials, the amount of equipment included in the base price. All are important when it comes to figuring the value of the house in terms of your particular taste, needs, and pocketbook.

25

HEATING AND PLUMBING

Whether to include some form of heat in your vacation house depends on where the house is located and how it is to be used. For most of the country you can get along without an expensive heating system if the house is to be used only during the warm summer months. If it is in a cool area and you want to use it in the early spring and into the fall, better consider heat. No matter where you live, if you want to use your vacation house in winter, better have heat—even if your house is in Florida.

ELECTRIC HEAT

As far as ease of installation and convenience go, electric heat is the ideal system for a vacation house. All that is needed, aside from electricity, are the units to provide heat in the rooms where it is needed. These units can be baseboard, wall, or panel types. In the latter the heating coils are concealed in the walls and ceilings. Resistance electric heating is not an expensive system to install; there is no need

208

to have a chimney, boiler, or furnace; and no servicing or maintenance is required. With electric heat you can go away for a week or longer in cold weather with the thermostat set at 55 degrees or so and be certain—barring a power failure—that the house will be comfortable when you return. And don't shy away from electric heat because of concern over a power failure, for any other kind of heating system—except a hand-fired coal furnace—will also go off when the power fails.

If you wish to cool your house in summer as well as heat it in winter, you can install window or wall reverse-cycle units that provide both heat and cooling. These are more expensive than other types of electric heat units but they do provide air conditioning.

Electric heat has some disadvantages, however, and it is not ideal everywhere for every kind of house. Unless you have a favorable electric rate, it can be a very expensive system to operate if you are going to heat the house all winter. Before you decide on electric heat, find out from your local utility or your electrical contractor what it is going to cost you a year to run the system. If you aren't sure whether this cost is high or low, get an estimate on what it will cost to operate an oil-fired system so you'll have some means of comparison.

Even with a favorable electric rate, electric heat can be very costly unless the house is built properly. A house that is to be heated by electric heat must be better insulated and tighter than one heated by other fuels. It needs thicker insulation in the roof, walls, and floors. It must have storm windows or insulating glass. It's got to be good and tight, and the more compact, the better. You can get by with a gas or oil-fired boiler or furnace in a poorly insulated, leaky sieve of a house, and though it will cost more to heat than if it were tight, it won't put you in the poorhouse. But if a house heated by electricity is not built for electric heat, you are in trouble.

Electric heat does better in a new house than in a remodeled one because in an old house it is not always possible to provide the amount of insulation and tightness of structure required for a good electric heat system.

GAS AND OIL

When it is not practical or economical to use electric heat, you will have to use gas or oil as a fuel for a central heating system. Which fuel to use depends on availability. As a rule, you aren't going to find gas lines in most vacation areas, which may rule gas out from the start. You can always get bottled gas, but to operate a central heating system on it is expensive.

Oil is the most common fuel for a vacation-house heating system since you can get it just about anyplace. You will need an oil storage tank, and if you live off the beaten track it's wise to put in a big one—a 550-gallon underground job—so that you'll always have plenty of oil on hand. This is especially important if you have a winter vacation house in a snow area, for oil delivery trucks can't always get through when you want them. It's also wise to put the tank as near a main road as practical. That way, even if your drive is ten feet under a snow drift, the delivery truck can reach the tank.

TYPES OF HEATING SYSTEMS

Gas or oil is used with either a circulating hot-water heating system or a forced warm-air system. A circulating hot-water system consists of a boiler to heat the water, a pump to circulate it through the system, and baseboard units, convectors, radiators, or coils in the floor or ceiling to provide heat to the various parts of the house. This is a good type of system, but it is more expensive than a forced warm-air system and it has the great disadvantage that, if the house is unheated at any time in freezing weather, the water in the system must either be drained or antifreeze added to it. This system also takes a little longer to bring the house up to a comfortable temperature than a forced warm-air type.

Forced warm-air systems are good if they are properly installed, and they cost less than the circulating hot-water system. Here you have registers in the floor or at the base of the walls to allow the heated air to flow into the rooms of the house. As the system does not contain water, there is no danger of damage to it from freezing and you get a very quick response when you turn up the thermostat.

If you don't mind putting up with something not quite so efficient, there is no need to go to the expense of installing a central heating system. In a small compact house, a floor furnace with one or two outlets costing around $350 can provide enough heat to keep the place warm. These run on either gas or oil and they can also be installed in walls. They do require a chimney. They are automatic and will keep the house warm even when it is not occupied. Fireplaces and wood stoves can also be used, as discussed in Chapter 27, "Fireplaces and Wood-burning Stoves."

PLUMBING SYSTEMS

We might as well start off by talking about how to get an adequate supply of fresh water. If you don't have this, the rest of the plumbing system isn't going to do you much good. There are several ways to get water. If you are on the shore of a lake or large pond, you can tap into this supply. If there is a spring or brook on the property that doesn't go dry at times, this may do the trick. You can also dig a well—a shallow one or a deep one depending on how much water you need and the depth of the water table on your site. Whatever the supply, it should be adequate to furnish around 300 gallons of water an hour. This is about what the average one-bathroom house requires when all the fixtures are in use at the same time.

Lakes and ponds.   These can provide a perfectly adequate supply of water if the water in them is not contaminated—and if it won't become contaminated in the future. You can have the water tested to find out if it's pure, but finding out if it will remain pure is something else again. About the only thing you can do on this score is to check with the local building and housing authorities to find out what provisions have been made to keep the water drinkable.

If the water is fit to use, it's a simple and inexpensive matter to tap into it. All you need is a shallow well pump costing under $200, some plastic pipe, and a foot valve that fits onto the end of the line and prevents water draining out of the system when the pump is not running. This system is fine as long as the water in the lake or pond doesn't freeze or you don't need water in winter because the house is closed. Installing this kind of system so that it will work when there is ice on the water gets complicated because the line has to run far enough out and deep enough so that it won't freeze.

Brooks and springs.   You can use the same type of equipment as for ponds and lakes. The trouble with brooks and springs is that they often go dry during a long dry spell and they can become contaminated if someone above you isn't careful with sewage.

Wells.   For most vacation houses a well is the most satisfactory means of getting a dependable supply of water. And by dependable we mean a flow of at least 5 gallons a minute which is about the minimum you can get along with in the typical vacation house today.

There are two types of wells: the shallow well and the deep well. The shallow well has a maximum depth of 25 feet. It can be drilled by a professional well driller or dug by hand. Compared to the deep well it is quite inexpensive. Such a well might cost less than $200 to have drilled or dug, and a pump suitable for it would be around $150. It is suitable, of course, only where the water table is rather close to the surface of the ground. The disadvantages of these wells is that they occasionally go dry during a long dry spell and sometimes they go dry permanently. This will happen if the water table drops because of a lot of new building in the area with each house drawing water out of the ground. Shallow wells are more easily contaminated than deep wells and should therefore be positioned a safe distance from septic systems.

Deep wells are wells that go below 25 feet. These wells tap water sources considerably below the surface and are not as apt to go dry as shallow wells. There is also less chance of the water being polluted. They cost considerably more than a shallow well. These wells must be drilled by professionals using special equipment. It may be necessary for them to go down several hundred feet to find a suitable supply of water. At $5.50 a foot, this can be pretty expensive. On top of the cost of drilling is the pump which will run around $300.

Which type of well will suit your needs depends on local conditions. You should check with your county agent, the state Water Resources Commission, and the local housing authorities to learn the approximate depth of water in your area and whether a shallow well is permitted. If you have to go to a deep well, keep in mind that no one can tell for sure how deep you will have to go before you strike an adequate supply of water. A good local well driller can give you a rough estimate, and you can ask the neighbors how far down they had to go, but each well is different and there is no way of knowing the depth of the well in advance.

SEWAGE

You are also going to need your own private sewage disposal system to handle the liquid waste from the house. This can be done with either a cesspool or septic tank but today most communities forbid cesspools and insist on a septic system.

Septic systems are installed by professionals who should first make a percolation test of the soil where the system is to be installed. This report may have to be passed on to the local housing and building authorities for their approval before work can begin. A septic system can run anywhere from $350 up, depending on soil conditions and the size of the system required. As we mentioned earlier, certain kinds of soil do not readily absorb liquids; in this case, if a septic system can be installed, it will cost far more than one in soil that is absorbent.

GAS AND CHEMICAL TOILETS

When it's not practical to have a septic system, or if your house doesn't have running water, you can still have an inside toilet. Gas and chemical toilets don't require either a sewer system or a water supply. Of the two, the gas toilet is the better but it's also the more expensive. This type of toilet operates on bottled gas and electricity. It is a combination toilet and incinerator. It can be installed inside the house but does require a vent to the outdoors. It is best, therefore, to have the bathroom on an outside wall or where the vent can be easily connected into an existing chimney.

This is the way a gas toilet works: When you raise the lid, it starts the exhaust blower and sets the time cycle. After use, you just close the lid and the incineration process begins. It will turn itself off automatically in ten minutes, but the toilet can be used during this interval. As soon as the lid is raised, the incineration process is interrupted and will begin again after the lid is lowered.

These units are perfectly safe for children. The seat does not get hot, there are no unpleasant odors, and one toilet can serve the daily requirements of twelve people. The only maintenance is periodic lubrication of the motor and removing the ashes by vacuuming. These units cost around $300.

Chemical toilets are considerably less expensive than the gas type and do not require electricity. But they should be vented. The waste matter must be emptied rather frequently. They cost around $175.

HOT WATER

The most convenient way to get hot water is with an automatic hot-water heater—electric, gas, or oil-fired. They all do a good job. If your house has electric heat or an electric kitchen range, chances are that you'll get a very good rate if you install an electric hot-water heater. The rate is not so good if you don't have electric heat or an electric range. Oil-fired heaters are excellent if you use oil for heating. Gas hot-water heaters use either natural or bottled gas. They have one advantage over the other types in that they will work even when there is no electricity.

For low-cost and rather primitive vacation houses you can get along with the old-fashioned kerosene hot-water heater. This consists of a kerosene burner, heating coil, and storage tank. The heater must be lighted in advance of when you want hot water and turned off when the water in the tank gets hot. The tank should be fitted with a safety valve to protect against explosion should you forget to turn off the heater.

An even less expensive way to get hot water is if you can find an old-fashioned wood or coal stove with a heating coil inside. This is connected to a storage tank, and as long as you've got a fire going in the stove, you'll have hot water in one degree or another.

26 GETTING ALONG WITHOUT ELECTRICITY

If your vacation-house site is way out in the boondocks, it may be impractical or expensive to bring in electric power—at least right away. Getting along without electricity can be an inconvenience, but it's no disaster. People in this country got along without electricity for years and lived quite happily.

One big plus in not having electricity is that it will save you a lot of money. You won't be tempted to buy expensive equipment and gadgets such as a dishwasher, garbage disposer, automatic washing machine and clothes dryer, freezer, vacuum cleaner, food blender, air conditioner, electric grill, and so forth. But you won't have to do without all modern conveniences. You can have a modern kitchen range that runs on bottled gas and even a gas automatic hot-water heater. For lights you can use battery-operated lamps or lamps that burn kerosene, gasoline, or bottled gas. The latter are less expensive to operate than the battery-operated type but they are something of a fire hazard.

For news of the outside world and entertainment you can have a battery-operated radio, TV, or even stereo system.

Refrigeration will be something of a problem because standard gas-burning refrigerators aren't manufactured anymore. Some small portable refrigerators operate on gas but, in addition to being small, they are rather expensive. There are also small refrigeration units that run off the electric power from an automobile. These cost from $80 to $200 depending on the size. You simply plug them into the cigarette lighter. They are primarily designed for camping, and how well they hold up under constant use is something we don't know.

If block ice is locally available you can use a modern version of the old-fashioned icebox. It won't keep food frozen but it will keep it cool. When we were young and lived out in the country, only the rich people had an icebox. Everybody else kept food cool either by lowering it into the well or having a coldbox down by the spring. Not many people are willing to go to that kind of trouble today—but it can still be done.

To have inside running water without electricity takes a bit of doing. What you need is something called a gravity system. This consists of a wood or metal storage tank set slightly higher than the highest point inside the house where you want running water, but not more than 20 feet higher than the location of the pump used to fill it. Twenty feet is as high as the average pump can make it. The tank should be open on the top and it can be set in the attic, on a tower away from the house, or even on a high piece of ground nearby. An outlet at the bottom of the tank is connected into the house water system. Once the pump has filled the tank, gravity does the rest, allowing the water to flow through the entire plumbing system. You can fill the tank either with a gasoline-driven pump or one worked by hand. But filling a large tank by hand takes a lot of work. A hand pressure pump runs around $20 and the gasoline-powered jobs about $150.

You won't have any problem with a sewage system if you have no electricity because it doesn't require anything but gravity. But automatic central heat is something else. You'll have to give that up if you have no electricity. You can use bottled gas heaters, but these are very expensive to operate unless they are used only occasionally. Kerosene space heaters are far less expensive to operate and they do a good job, but they should be vented into a chimney and many communities forbid them. Wood- and coal-burning stoves are excellent, and once you get the trick of them they don't require too much attention.

GENERATE YOUR OWN ELECTRICITY

What a lot of people do who can't bring power to their vacation houses but who still want electricity is to have their own electric power plant. Home-generating systems are operated by gasoline or bottled-gas motors. The gasoline types are used when the system is to be installed outside the house—in a garage or outbuilding. The slightly more expensive systems that run on bottled gas can be installed inside the house—in the basement, for example.

The capacity of these systems is measured in the number of watts the system will produce. Wattage also determines the cost. A small portable generator that can turn out 1,500 watts—enough to run a refrigerator or freezer—costs around $125. The large 5,000-watt home generators which have the capacity to handle just about all the electrical requirements except electric heat run between $700 and $800.

The big drawback to these systems is that you only get electricity when the generator is running. Small generating units are started by hand like a power lawn mower. The more expensive types have a self-starter such as you have in a car. And if you are willing to pay for it, you can have a system that turns on as soon as there is a demand for electricity. In other words, if you have a freezer, the generator will go on by itself as soon as the freezer decides that it needs electricity. Pretty smart!

As the cost of a generator is based on its output, the thing to do is to get the smallest one able to handle essentials. For most vacation houses these essentials would include the water pump, refrigerator, and possibly a freezer and washing machine. You may also want to use electricity for lighting, but if you do, the generator will have to run until the last light is turned off at night. And then, unless it is the superautomatic type, someone has to go out and shut off the engine. Also, they do make something of a racket.

Right after World War II we lived through a winter with a small, 750-watt generator. We used it for the water pump, refrigerator, and oil burner. It scarcely had the capacity to handle even one of these pieces of equipment at a time, but we had all sorts of special switches and wiring so that we could feed power to each piece as it was needed. In the morning we'd first run up the oil burner to warm the house, and when that was finished we'd switch on the pump, and when that turned off we'd give the refrigerator a little juice. We'd repeat this process several times each day. We made it through the winter, but we got pretty sick and tired of starting that generator.

You can buy generating systems through local electric contractors or direct from mail-order houses such as Sears, Roebuck and Montgomery Ward. There is one kind of home generator, by the way, that can be connected under the hood to the engine of a car but this is primarily for emergency use.

Generating equipment should be installed by a qualified electrician and the wiring inside the house should be of the same quality as that required for regular electric service. If you are building or remodeling, it is worth the expense to have adequate wiring installed, even if you aren't going to use it at the time. When and if you do get centrally generated power, it will be a simple matter to connect the existing house wiring to the main lines. If, however, the house is completed and then you decide to have it wired, it's going to cost a good deal of money.

27 FIREPLACES AND WOOD-BURNING STOVES

We'd almost rather go without inside plumbing in a vacation house than without a fireplace or some form of wood-burning unit. An indoor wood fire and a vacation house just go together, regardless of the climate. On a cool day or evening the fire will help take the chill off, and on a wet or dreary day it will provide cheer. We've enjoyed the special pleasures of an open fire on a balmy evening in the Florida Keys, on a cool evening in the hills of southern California, on a wet day on a beach in Oregon, and on many a bitter cold night in Minnesota, New England, and the Texas Panhandle. You've just got to have some wood-burning unit in your vacation house. Fortunately, there is some kind of fireplace or wood-burning stove to fit almost every budget—even one under $100.

Some wood-burning units—such as an ordinary fireplace—are designed primarily to provide cheer; others, such as parlor stoves, are designed primarily to provide heat. But the two functions are not mutually exclusive: a fireplace also provides a certain amount of heat, and we've spent many a cheerful hour toasting our feet by a parlor stove.

220

FIREPLACES

Masonry fireplaces. Even though they aren't too efficient in supplying heat to a room, masonry fireplaces are hard to beat. They can be the most attractive of all wood-burning units—and also the most expensive. If you decide to have one built of local stone it can cost, if not an arm and a leg, at least several thousands of dollars. Unless you get fancy, a brick fireplace will cost considerably less—under $1,000.

Building a masonry fireplace so that the chimney draws properly and the fireplace doesn't smoke is still something of an art. Even though standards have been established to give the proper ratios between the fireplace opening, depth of firepit, and area of throat and flue, fireplaces that don't work right still get built. We don't recommend your doing this job yourself, and we also don't recommend hiring a mason to build a fireplace for you unless he has had some experience and you have checked with other homeowners and found that the fireplaces he has built are good. Nothing is so useless and frustrating as a fireplace that can't be used because it smokes up the house.

A fireplace can be placed so that the chimney runs through the house or on an outside wall. An inside chimney is usually the better of the two because it doesn't get as cold as an outside one and therefore often draws better. Also, if a fire is kept burning pretty steadily, the inside chimney will give off some heat to the house while an outside one wastes the heat on the outdoors.

Modified fireplaces. These are manufactured fireplace units sometimes called "circulating fireplaces." They are made. of heavy steel and are set in place and then covered by stone or brick. The steel unit contains all the essential parts of a fireplace—firepit, damper, throat, smoke shelf, and chamber. As the units are properly designed and factory built, they function perfectly if provided with a chimney of the correct area and height. Another advantage is that the units have an air chamber in the rear so that as cold air flows through openings at the bottom, it is heated by passing across the warm metal in back of the fire, and then discharged through outlets at the top of the unit.

Modified fireplaces are good if you plan to build the fireplace yourself, cannot get an experienced fireplace mason, or want to get the maximum amount of heat out of your fireplace.

It is amazing how much heat these units will generate after a fire has been burning in them for a few hours. If you wish, ducts can be connected to the hot-air outlets on the unit and run to other areas of the house. Or the hot air can be discharged into the same room through vents in the front or side of the fireplace. With a good fire going, one of these large units can keep a small compact vacation house warm even in very cold weather.

Modified fireplace units range from around $250 up, depending on their size. Their only drawback, in our opinion, is that the inside of the fireplace is steel rather than the more attractive firebrick. But once the metal has become coated with soot, it's hard to tell that the inside is not masonry.

A modified fireplace may increase the overall cost of a fireplace slightly, especially if you are using a skilled mason, but if you have someone who is not too familiar with fireplace construction, the time saved in not having to work out the necessary proportions will often equal the cost of the unit.

Prefabricated fireplaces.   These are great. They are made of metal and come with a prefabricated metal chimney. They can be put up in a matter of a few hours, don't require any foundation or footings, and can be set against a wall or in the middle of a room. Best of all, they don't cost much. Since they don't weigh much either, you can even stick one in a second-floor bedroom if you like.

Prefabricated fireplaces come in a variety of styles, sizes, and prices that start at around $350 for a good-quality unit. The chimney, which is simply hung on the roof rafters or floor joists, is approved by the Underwriters Laboratories and perfectly safe. You need a base of some noncombustible material for the unit. A good solution is a box made of 2 by 4s on edge filled with gravel or marble chips. It's quite possible to install a prefab fireplace and chimney yourself. Most units come with complete installation instructions.

Prefabricated fireplaces are never very large, so if your idea of a fireplace is to have something capable of handling the traditional Yule log—forget the prefab and go to masonry. But if all you want is a nice cheerful fireplace that will toss out a bit of heat, prefabs are an excellent buy. Although most building codes permit these units, a few don't, so check your local situation before you buy.

STOVES

By our definition, a stove is a wood- or coal-burning unit in which the flames are enclosed on all sides. Stoves give off more heat than fireplaces, and you can burn odd-size chunks of wood in them as well as coal. What's more, by opening or closing the damper on the chimney, or those on the stove itself, you can control the rate of burning to some degree.

Stoves, too, come in all sizes and shapes. There are the old-fashioned cast-iron stoves that look pretty much like the ones that came out of the back of the general store one hundred years ago, and there are stoves with more contemporary styling. There are round stoves, square ones, short ones, and high ones. Some are designed for other purposes besides heating the room. The old-fashioned kitchen stove not only warms the room but can simmer a stew like no other kitchen range. The laundry stove, designed to heat a large container of water for the family wash, can be used to heat water for washing dishes or even bathing. And then there is the famous Franklin stove, which is a sort of cross between a fireplace and a stove.

Stoves are relatively inexpensive. You can get a new one of good design for around $90, but you can also pick up plain units for under $50. And you can get some good buys at secondhand furniture places and junk stores.

Stoves are easy to install. They can be supported by any

solid floor, though it's always smart to put some nonflammable materials under the stove legs and on the adjacent area. That way, if a spark does jump out, it won't harm the floor. Metal, asbestos board, or masonry will do. The stove should also be set far enough away from a wall so that the wall does not become overheated.

Stoves can be connected to a masonry or prefabricated metal chimney, but they do need a flue of their own. If you run the stove into the same flue as the fireplace, chances are one or the other or both will smoke or otherwise operate improperly. In a new installation, the least expensive chimney for a stove is one made of concrete chimney blocks. But it is ugly. If we couldn't afford a chimney of brick or stone, we'd prefer the more expensive prefabricated metal chimney to one of concrete block.

A stove or two can heat a small vacation house quite adequately. For this kind of use, coal is a better fuel than wood. Once you get the trick of it, you can keep the stove going day and night with a minimum of effort.

In country stores or shops where they still use wood or coal stoves for heating, you'll often notice that the stove is sitting a long way from the chimney with a long run of stovepipe connecting the two. The idea here is that the stovepipe, once it gets warm, gives off a good deal of heat. If you are planning on using a stove to heat your vacation house, that's a good thing to remember.

FUEL FOR FIREPLACES AND STOVES

If you are using wood for fuel, the best kind of wood is hardwood such as oak, maple, or birch. These woods give off a lot of heat with a minimum amount of smoke. Softwoods such as pine, balsam, and fir burn faster than hardwood and give off a lot of smoke. Seasoned wood, of course, always burns better than unseasoned stuff.

28 WOOD DECKS

A wooden deck or two has become pretty standard equipment for vacation houses. They give a lot of pleasure for the money. Even a simple deck improves the appearance of most houses, and they can make a small house seem a lot larger than it is and even act larger. If you place the deck around an entry walk, it will help keep a lot of dirt, sand, and debris out of the house. And, of course, decks are good to sit on.

A wood deck is more expensive to build than a plain concrete terrace. A run-of-the-mill deck will run around $2.50 a square foot before you are finished whereas you can get a concrete terrace for around 50 cents a square foot, provided the ground is level and the concrete can be poured with a minimum of fill and forms. If the area around the house is uneven, the cost goes up for concrete; and if the house is on a slope, concrete is out of the question.

In hot weather a wood deck is cooler than a concrete terrace; it is easier to keep clean; and it will dry faster in wet weather. To our mind it is also more attractive.

The least expensive deck to build is one with only one level. When you get into multilevel decks, or decks with conversation pits, you get into a lot more money—not only for materials but

225

for labor. And unless you are going to build the deck yourself, it will cost less to have it done when the house is built than to add it on later. The best decks are those that are planned at the same time as the house and therefore become an integral part of the design.

Decks are usually made out of redwood, cedar, or Douglas fir. Redwood is the most durable but also the most expensive. You can reduce the cost of a redwood deck if you use the construction grade in place of the more costly, clear all-heart redwood. Cedar is somewhat less expensive than redwood and Douglas fir is the least expensive of all.

You can use either 2-by-3, 2-by-4, or 2-by-6 stock for the decking. The first two can be laid on edge as well as on face. When decking is laid on face, the bark side of the boards should be up. The wood won't absorb moisture as easily that way as it would if the boards were laid upside down with the concave side of the growth rings facing up.

Decking should be fastened with aluminum, stainless steel, or high-quality hot-dipped galvanized nails. Don't use ordinary steel nails because they will rust and stain the wood, and they will eventually fail. The boards used for decking should be spaced 1/4 inch apart.

Never paint a wood deck. Paint has to be renewed rather frequently when used for this purpose, but more important, it can encourage decay in the wood. Redwood does not normally require any treatment and will weather with age to an attractive color. Other woods can be treated with a water repellent or a clear wood preservative. If the wood isn't too attractive and you'd like to add a bit of color and ensure an even finish, use an exterior preservative stain. A "bleaching oil" is excellent for wood decks. It acts as a preservative for woods and also hastens the natural bleaching to produce a driftwood effect in the space of a few months.

All wood portions of the deck should be treated with a water repellent, preservative, or stain with the exception of decks made of clear all-heart redwood. If you want to do a first-class job, treat each piece of wood before it is installed. Any woodwork that comes into direct contact with the ground should be pressure-treated with a wood preservative to protect it from decay and insects. Wood treated in this way can be purchased from a lumber yard.

29 PROTECTING YOUR HOUSE AGAINST ILLEGAL ENTRY

A modest vacation house that is closed for the season does not attract the professional burglar. He knows from previous experience that the family has probably taken all their valuables with them when they left. On the other hand, vacation houses, especially in remote areas, are attractive to vandals who destroy property "just for kicks," and vacation houses are also attractive to young people—often from the best of families—who want an out-of-the-way spot for a party or to spend a weekend. If they happen to find something in the house they would like to have, they will naturally take it; and if there is liquor about, they will naturally drink it. Even houses in built-up communities are visited by both vandals and this latter group of pleasure seekers.

The best way to protect a house when it is unoccupied is to board it up. Lock all doors and windows and then install solid shutters of wood or metal on every window and door. The shutters should be securely fastened to the inside of the window and door frame with long wood screws so that they can be removed only by a major effort and a lot of time and noise.

The next-best protection are locks on doors and windows that can't be picked or otherwise opened without a special key.

228

For a solid outside door, a dead-bolt lock is good. If the door has glass panels in it, which is often the case with side or back doors, you will need the type of dead-bolt lock that can't be opened from the inside or the outside without a key. Otherwise, all someone has to do is smash a pane of glass, reach inside, and open the lock.

Sliding glass doors should be locked or secured in some other way. Wedge-locks are available that can be used if the door did not come with a keyed lock but simply a latch. Sliding doors can also be made inoperable once closed by putting a length of wood dowel in the channel in which the door slides.

Ordinary window latches don't offer much in the way of protection, but they are better than nothing. A better safeguard is to install keyed wedge locks on all windows. These can't be opened even if a pane of glass is smashed and the intruder can reach inside.

Burglar alarms are useful, especially if they are the right type, by which we mean the type that are wired into a central station or to the local police station. With this type of alarm, when an intruder breaks into the house the police are immediately notified and can come over to see what the trouble is all about. This type of system is only practical, however, when the house is fairly close to the police station. If a policeman has to drive five miles over winding dirt roads to get from police headquarters to your house, chances are the intruder will have left before he arrives.

Another kind of alarm system is the local one that just gives out a loud ring. If there are occupied houses in the area near enough to hear the sound of the alarm, this system may be of help. Otherwise, an intruder isn't going to worry much about the noise.

Don't leave anything around the grounds that might look attractive to someone with a roving eye. For example, unless small boats and canoes are locked up or securely chained with a good padlock, they often disappear during the off season. Larger boats are often stripped of anything of value—even an inboard engine.

Regardless of what else you do to protect your house when it is unoccupied, notify the local or state police when you close up for the season. They can then post the property and make frequent inspections that will help prevent trouble. You should also notify any nearby neighbors so that they, too, can keep an eye on your place.

RENTING
YOUR HOUSE

With varying degrees of success, many families ease the financial strain of owning a vacation house by renting it out at certain times of the year. Many of the new, planned vacation communities even promote this concept as a sales inducement: "We can almost guarantee that we can rent your house at any time you don't require it for your own use."

There's no doubt about it. The right house in the right location can bring in a whopping amount of money in rent. Even a shack, if it's in a desirable spot, can earn a handsome rental. There are also tax advantages, because although rent is income and taxable as such, repairs and some of the cost incurred in getting the house ready for tenants are deductible items. The deductions will not exceed the income, but the incentive to keep the house well equipped and in good repair is considerable. If you don't have your own accountant, you can get expert advice from the Internal Revenue Service on the tax laws applicable to rental properties.

But renting does have drawbacks. Before you buy or build a vacation house with the notion of renting it, consider all the factors involved and find out what you can expect in the way of rentals at the season or time you would be willing to give the place up.

When it comes down to the wire, are you really willing to rent? Lots of families chicken out when the moment to put their house on the market actually arrives. It's one thing to talk about renting when you are still in the planning stage, but once you have moved in and begun to enjoy your house, leaving it to the mercy of strangers is a hard thing to do. It's especially no fun if you are not going off on some other form of vacation but have to sweat out the summer in the city or suburbs.

You also have to think through how you will feel about renting many of your possessions to people you don't even know. Some families have found that once they turned house and belongings over to someone else, they were no longer theirs in the sense they had been before. It can often take a bit of brightness out of the place to return to it knowing that someone else has had parties on your deck or terrace, has enjoyed your view, cooked in your kitchen, slept in your bed, and used your personal possessions. This is one reason why families who rent their houses regularly furnish them in a rather impersonal fashion.

Summer tenants are hard on a house. For some reason the wear and tear on a vacation house is much more than on a year-round place. And it doesn't seem to matter who the tenants are. Some of the most attractive and responsible people may treat a vacation house in a rather casual manner. If they're disagreeable and irresponsible, they'll treat it very badly. With this type of tenant, you can be sure that, when you return, the house is going to be considerably the worse for wear. Surprisingly so-called nice people will sometimes even take off with a particular object or book that strikes their fancy. This is another reason why a family that regularly rents will furnish their house with pieces of minor value and won't leave any of their dearest belongings about.

HOW MUCH CAN YOU GET?

What price you can get for a vacation house depends on its location. As is true of land values, a tiny cabin on the beach or by a lake or river can bring in more than an attractive and comfortable house that is far from recreational areas. And *when* you rent is also important. In the northern states a lakeside or seaside cottage is worth a lot of money in the summer months but practically nothing the day after Labor Day. In the South it's just the other way around: winter rentals are good and summer rentals poor. A house near the ski slopes can be rented easily in winter, but if there are no summer recreational facilities nearby, renting in warm weather may be a problem.

What all this comes down to is that your place will be most valuable as a rental property at the time you want it for yourself. Yet some families have found ways to beat the system. One family we know built a ski house even though they don't particularly like to ski. What they do enjoy is hiking. So they rent their place out in winter for a top rental and enjoy it themselves all summer. Another family rents their large beach house for July and August for $2,000 a month. They take their own vacation in September and enjoy the place on weekends the rest of the year. Because they don't have school-age children the system works out fine.

As a general rule, we would say that if you have children, renting your vacation house in July and August is not realistic. Still, if you are in a bind financially, you may have to rent whether you want to or not. In that case, think of the house as a property that will help pay off your loan so that some day you can have the place all to yourself. In the meantime it's a weekend place where you can also go for a week or two in June after school lets out.

In spite of the general demand for rental property, you can't always be dead sure of renting your place at your price every year. A dip in the economy can have a great effect on the rental market. When things get a little tight, one of the easiest ways a family can economize is to cut down on their vacation expenses, and when they do cut down it can leave you with an empty house or with having to rent it for much less that you originally planned.

No matter how or when you plan to rent, we recommend checking with a local real estate broker to find out what's what. Tell him the locale of the house, its size, when and for how long you're prepared to rent it, and other pertinent information. He can then give you a pretty good idea of what sort of money you will be able to get. He will probably charge you an appraiser's fee for this service, unless you employ him as your agent to find those satisfactory tenants. You might also check in with the local bank, and it's always wise to look through the classified real estate ads in the local newspapers to see what rents are being asked for properties similar to yours.

HOW TO FIND A SATISFACTORY TENANT

What sort of tenant you can get depends on your location. If your vacation house is near a year-round community, you may be able to rent to a young couple who haven't reached the point where they can afford to build a house of their own. Also, in areas with year-round residents, you can often pick up tenants who are waiting while their own house is being built or who are looking over the community before commiting themselves to buy. Retired couples, too, may be potential renters during an off season. In any event, don't count on schoolteachers as nine-months' tenants. Everyone and his brother has had the same idea, and there simply aren't enough schoolteachers to go around.

The simplest way to get a satisfactory tenant is to turn the job over to a local real estate broker. These are the ones that people looking for rental property naturally turn to, so a broker will usually have a substantial list of prospective tenants. If you ask a broker to rent your property he'll charge you a commission of around 10 percent. You can, of course, find your own tenants—friends or someone you have heard of who is looking for a house. But under ordinary conditions, dealing through a broker is your best bet.

HOW TO BE A LANDLORD

If you own a vacation house and decide to rent it, there are several ways to be a landlord. The simplest is to turn the entire operation over to a management concern. They will help you determine what rent you can get, find you a tenant if there is one to be had, handle the lease, collect the rent, and even oversee maintenance and repairs on the property. With this arrangement you can go away—and stay away for years if you wish—knowing that your property will be cared for. If you want the whole matter out of your hair and can afford the commission—sometimes up to 25 percent of the rent—this is the arrangement to have.

Many planned vacation communities have management groups of this type who handle the houses in that particular development. You'll also find management concerns in many vacation areas handling individual houses scattered around the region. Many real estate brokers also provide this kind of service. Even when a broker is not set up to handle all phases of property management, he can provide a good many services if you rent your property through him. He'll find you a tenant, draw up the lease, arrange for payments to be made, and also keep an eye on your house so that it is properly maintained. You can, of course, handle the entire operation yourself—find your own tenant, make the necessary financial arrangements, and be a combination superintendent, handyman, and gentle adviser.

The role of landlord is not easy—particularly when you are

renting a vacation house. Tenants can be awfully dumb about the operation of a house, especially if they are from the city. They'll use water the way they use it in the city and pretty soon the well runs dry. They'll forget that they may have to order bottled gas and pretty soon they run out of gas. Unless you spell everything out for them, you may find they are constantly on the telephone with questions and complaints about mechanical or aesthetic problems, or even—surprising as it may seem— about the neighbor's children or social contretemps.

Before you turn over your house to a tenant, take him around and explain how everything works and what he will be required to do to keep it working. And to be on the safe side, write it all down and leave these instructions with him. Give him the names and telephone numbers of the servicemen he may need—the plumber, electrician, gas man, etc. Make a complete inventory of every essential item in the house and give one copy to the tenant and keep another for yourself.

Families who regularly rent their vacation homes will tell you that while you can get more money renting by the week or month to several tenants, the wear and tear on the house—not to mention on you—is far greater than if you have a single tenant for the entire period. And if several families occupy the house, it's more difficult to determine which one is responsible for damages to the property. Finally, each time the house is vacated you must come in—or have someone else come in—to clean it up and make it fresh for the next tenant.

31 INSURANCE FOR YOUR VACATION HOUSE

What kind of insurance you can get and what it will cost depends on where your vacation house is located. If it's in the wrong place or is the wrong kind of house, you may not be able to get the protection you want—not at any reasonable premium, that is.

One type of insurance you won't have trouble getting is liability coverage. This is the type you need to protect you if someone other than a member of the family gets hurt on your property because of some negligence on your part. It is particularly important to have this coverage on your vacation house because people are more apt to get hurt when they play than when they are just sitting around.

The other important kinds of coverage are fire, theft, and windstorm. If your house is in a settled community that has adequate fire and police protection, this coverage is easy to obtain. This is especially true in a good planned vacation development where additional security is often provided by the community and where any damage to your house, even when you are not around, will be attended to immediately, so that the damage is held to a minimum. But it may not be so easy to get adequate coverage at a reasonable rate if your house is in a remote area and at a considerable distance from the nearest

237

fire or police department. In this case your premiums for fire insurance are going to be very high.

And the same thing holds true of theft insurance. By the way, as far as theft insurance goes, be sure you have enough coverage so that it includes all the gear found around a vacation house—boats, motors, sporting equipment, and so forth. (If you can get it at all.)

If you are building near the water, remember that the standard home fire insurance policy will not protect your house from damage by water. It will protect you from windstorm, but only from damage to the house that is a direct result of the wind. In other words, if the wind blows the roof off the house, you are covered. If the wind drives the water up over your house and washes it away, you are out of luck. You are particularly out of luck if you have a mortgage on the house because you are going to have to pay off that mortgage loan even if the house no longer exists. There was a sad case some years ago in which someone had built a house on a little strip of land that ran between the ocean and a bay. A hurricane came along and not only washed the house away but the land too. Naturally, no insurance covered this, and the owner had only recently purchased the house and with a sizable mortgage loan.

There is a type of federal disaster insurance that is available in some areas to cover this kind of situation. But the local community has to make application first; only after the claim is approved for the area can the individual home owner get protection from water damage.

32 CLOSING THE HOUSE FOR THE SEASON

If you don't want to come back next season to a disaster, take the time and effort to close your place properly before you leave it at the end of the season. Try not to leave any items of great value in the house because if you do have an unwelcome intruder when you are away, he may take them with him. This is especially true of small objects of value that are easily carried and have a wide appeal such as radios, TV, sporting equipment, and so forth. If you can't remove them from the house, put them in a closet that has a good lock on the door.

It's best to take, give, or throw away all foodstuffs with the exception of those that won't be harmed by freezing or lack of refrigeration. Packaged cereals, breadcrumbs, macaroni, and other dry foods attract rodents and should be stored in tight metal containers if they are to be left. The refrigerator and freezer should be turned off, emptied, and cleaned thoroughly. The refrigerator door should be left open so that it won't become musty inside. An open package of charcoal helps keep the interior fresh-smelling.

Bedding, towels, etc., should be washed or dry cleaned before storing them away. For homes on the seashore or near lakes where dampness can be a problem, it's wise to leave as few articles as possible. What can't be removed should be hung up, rather than packed away, to get the maximum amount of air and sunshine. Beds should be stripped so that the mattress gets plenty of ventilation.

Mice, rats, squirrels, and other rodents find a summer house a pleasant place to spend the winter. It will help reduce the rodent problem if you have nothing inside the house that will attract them. Food is an obvious lure but if they are hungry they will eat candles, soap, and sponges. If you use self-striking matches, be sure to store them in metal containers as a rodent can set one off if be begins to nibble on it.

Seal up any openings on the outside of your house that might allow rodents to get inside. Fill any cracks or holes in the foundation with concrete. Get some metal collars at your hardware store and use them to cover the seam where water pipes run through floors and outside walls. Also remove any branches that are close to the house. By jumping from a nearby branch, squirrels and other climbing rodents often can enter a house through openings along the eaves.

Be sure that everything on the outside of the house is secure —the shutters and the TV aerial, for example—and don't leave objects outdoors if you can help it. A heavy wind can toss outdoor furniture around and damage it or allow it to damage the house. During the winter months, tides can be especially high and will wash away objects that during the mild weather are perfectly safe. Lakes, rivers, and brooks have a bad habit of running over their banks at certain times of the year.

DRAINING THE PLUMBING

If your house is located in an area where temperatures drop below freezing, everything inside the house that can be damaged by cold must be either removed or, in the case of plumbing, drained.

If you have a local plumber, he can drain the system for you and put it back in operation in the spring. For an average vacation house the charge for this might be $20 or $30 each visit. If you don't have a plumber who can do this for you, you'll have to do it yourself. And if you do it yourself, be thorough. If you leave water in one line of pipe or fixture trap, you may have some expensive repair work next season.

First, turn off the water supply by shutting off the pump. If you happen to get your water from a water main, the water company will come around and turn it off for you. Open all the faucets in the house. Drain the water out of the pump—there is a little drain plug at the base which you can remove with a wrench. Drain the water out of the storage tank and the hot-water heater. When you drain these tanks and lines be sure the faucets in the house are opened because if they aren't, a partial vacuum will form that will prevent complete drainage. You can drain the storage and hot-water tanks into buckets or pails, but a good deal of water may be involved, so it's easier to connect a garden hose to the drain faucet and let the water flow outdoors.

Now you have to drain the cold-and hot-water lines. In a well-designed modern plumbing system, these lines are given a slight downward pitch and at the lowest point of each line there will be a drain valve, or a shut-off valve. To drain the line, open the drain valves, or turn the little knurled knob on each shut-off valve. Open the knobs on any other shut-off valves in the system to drain the water out of these valves as well as the adjoining pipes.

In older systems you may find a length of horizontal pipe with no downward pitch. This allows water to remain in the pipes even when the drain valve is opened. What you have to do in this case is disconnect these lines where you find a union so that they can be drained.

The drainage or waste system is not complicated to winterize, for the only place water collects is in the traps. For sinks, bathtubs, showers, and lavatories, pour a quart of kerosene slowly down the drain. It will replace the water in the trap and prevent freezing; it will also stop sewer gas from coming into the house. Flush the toilet to empty the tank and sponge out water remains in the tank and the bowl. Add about two quarts of kerosene to the bowl. If you have an electric dishwasher or washing machine, follow the manufacturer's directions for draining.

You'll also have to remove from the house any items that might freeze. These include canned and bottled goods from the pantry shelf, ink, latex paint, and so forth. Don't leave any water in glass or pottery flower vases; if the water inside them freezes, the vases will crack.

33 THE HAPPY VACATION HOUSE

There's more to having a happy vacation house than its location, design, and size. How much you will enjoy your second home also depends on your furnishings and your approach to vacation living.

First, unless you are merely looking for a status symbol, it doesn't make much difference in what style you furnish a vacation house. Sure, make the house gay and attractive. Try to make it as different as possible from your primary home— whether that is an apartment or a house. Right down to sheets, towels, and other necessities, try to have different colors and patterns in each. One of the reasons for a vacation house is to have a change, and a visual change can be as important as one of environment.

Keep your furnishings casual and inexpensive. What's the point of leaning over backward to build or buy a vacation house that keeps the family budget in one piece and then blowing it to bits on furniture? There is also no point in furnishing a vacation house in such a way that it is going to need constant time, effort, and worry on your part to maintain. Vacation living can be hard on furniture—especially if there are a lot of kids about, if you rent the place from time to time, or if you are in a remote area where the house may be broken into.

You don't need to spend a fortune making a vacation house attractive and comfortable. Get the simplest, most inexpensive contemporary furniture available. The unfinished kind is the least expensive good stuff and it's easy to finish, either with a couple of coats of paint or with one of the very durable wood sealers that are heat- and liquor-resistant. You get the best buys in this kind of furniture through mail-order houses or in specialty shops.

Another way to furnish on a budget is with good paintable secondhand pieces. As long as the pieces are solid, or can be made solid with glue, all it takes to give them a new lease on life is a coat or two of paint. We know of many families who have furnished their vacation homes for peanuts with pieces they've picked up for $5, $15, and $25 at secondhand furniture shops, garage and barn sales, local auctions, and junk yards. Even the town dump can be a good source of used furniture, but you've got to get there early in the morning before the "bargains" have disappeared into the back of some fancy station wagon.

Make shopping and scrounging for used furniture a family affair. Once they get the idea of what you are looking for, children can turn up some great bargains and they are not the least bit hesitant about crawling around in the back of a dusty used furniture shop or the town dump. And kids are more apt to keep their room in some sort of shape if they have had a hand in selecting and painting their own furniture.

Save yourself a lot of money by using natural accessories about the house—rocks, pieces of driftwood, shells, pine cones, and other objects that you can find in the woods or by the shore.

The one place you should spend money is for good beds. Skimp on everything else that goes into the house but don't cheat the family out of a decent night's sleep. What you do about your guests' beds is your own affair. The guest who sleeps on a bed that feels like a pile of stones seldom overstays his or her welcome.

Unless you want to spend all your time keeping house and cleaning up, stay away from heavy carpeting, upholstery that soils easily, and anything else that requires constant care or that you worry about breaking or ruining.

Select slipcovers, curtains, draperies that are pre-pressed and can be washed rather than dry cleaned. Remember, also, that when the house is closed for any extended period, you can expect small visitors who can do considerable damage to a variety of objects. Field mice won't hesitate to rip the fibers out of your rugs and carpets to make a nest and rats and squirrels will gnaw through just about anything if they believe it will gain them a crumb of food.

The whole point is not to let the house and its maintenance run *you*. You are there for pleasure and relaxation, and you should run the house as little as possible.

EQUIPMENT

Have two of everything you can possibly afford; if you can't afford two of everything, make do without when you're in your vacation house. Anything to avoid the constant shuttling back and forth of such things as a vacuum cleaner, iron, or Dutch oven. There is nothing more nerve-wracking than trying to remember everything you have to take with you each time you change houses. Make it simple and keep it simple.

If you can afford a washer-dryer, your laundry problems are simplified. You'll also have a place to dry wet swimsuits and beach towels, not to mention ski clothes. If you can't afford a washer-dryer, try to get a local laundry service. By all means try to avoid having to take soiled clothes back to the city or having to spend several hours each weekend at the local laundromat.

We have found that many families consider an automatic dishwasher more important for a vacation house than for their primary residence. If you have one or plan to get one, be sure that all your cooking and service gear can be tossed into it without harm. Vacation living, by the way, is very hard on kitchen and serving items such as pots, pans, cups, glasses, spoons, forks, and so on. If they can break, they will break sooner or later—and usually sooner. If they are small, sooner or later they'll get lost in the sand or among the pine needles, and if they are handy they will be appropriated for essential jobs like bailing out the boat, or for use as a container for bait or a baking dish for mud pies. Don't have anything around that will break your heart if it disappears or gets broken.

A good rule to follow in buying mechanical equipment for a vacation house is to buy the best but not necessarily the fancy stuff. The more complex an appliance, the more chance there is for it getting out of whack. For impartial ratings of appliances you can't beat *Consumer's Report.* Also, for standard items such as dishwashers, washer-dryers and refrigerators, be sure to buy brands that can be serviced locally. If you have a favorite brand but there is no one within a hundred miles who can service it, you'll have a lot of trouble when it goes on the blink.

FOOD

The trick here is to spend as little time marketing as possible. And avoid shopping on weekends as you would the plague. Aside from the fact that to shop weekends is a dull event at best, stores in vacation areas are packed with people at this time and you can kill half a day standing in line at the checkout counter. Remember, too, that in most vacation communities, the price of food is higher than you may be accustomed to and the variety is limited. If you are going to be at your vacation house for any extended period, it's worth making a trip to a nearby large community and laying in a good stock of supplies.

If you are in an area where power failures are *not* frequent you can keep a good supply of food in a freezer, but to be really safe, keep plenty of canned food around. Try to buy your staples in quantity, once a month or so, so that you're not constantly having to run to a market that may be a good many miles away.

Look for local goodies (hams, jellies, chickens, eggs, and so forth). In summer either feast on your own home-grown vegetables or find a nearby farm where you can get the bounty of the season whether it's early June peas, fresh corn, or crisp fall apples. Almost every area has regional foods that are a delight to discover and a feast to eat.

VACATION LIVING

The more you learn about what's around you, the more you'll enjoy your vacation house and your time at it. It's fine to pursue your particular pastime—whether it's golf, skiing, boating, or fishing—but you'll get infinitely more out of your place if you take an interest in other areas and explore them a bit. If you're not familiar with *The Last Whole Earth Catalog,* buy a copy at your local bookstore. It is brimful of all kinds of lore, advice and—if you're receptive—helpful comments and ruminations about country living. If you're a young adult you probably already know about this unusual and fascinating book. If you're a parent of young adults you ought to know about it. Parent or nonparent, read this book and you'll discover a lot about what the younger generation is doing and thinking and how they are solving many of the same problems you will be facing—and solving.

Learn about the animals and vegetation in your area. You'll enjoy life much more if you are familiar with the various species of birds that may visit your place, the kinds of reptiles you may encounter on a walk, and the names of the various trees, plants, and shrubs. Some of the paperback books on these subjects are excellent for beginners, and once you get the bug you can move on to more advanced works.

Plant a cutting garden so you'll have fresh flowers for the house. This kind of garden doesn't take much attention, and if you are from the city you'll delight in being able to fill vase after vase with fresh-cut flowers that don't cost you a dime.

Watch your socializing! Unless you are happiest when you are in a crowd, try not to get too involved with parties. Before you know it, you'll be in as much of a social whirl, complete with obligations to repay hospitality, as you are in your year-round home. You don't have to be a hermit, but the whole idea is to get back to a simpler way of living, isn't it?

Take your time making friends. Don't latch on to the first family you meet and don't let them latch on to you because after you really get to know them, you may find they are not all that attractive. The ideal situation is to have a lot of nice neighbors—but neighbors rather than friends. It's a big nuisance if each time you entertain you feel obligated to invite the family next door just because they happen to live next door and will have their feelings hurt if they see you out in back drinking and eating with others and you haven't invited them. If you really want privacy, fences around your outdoor living area can help reduce the neighbor problem, but put them up when you first buy or build to avoid hurt feelings.

Above all, keep reminding yourself that what you have is a vacation house and the whole idea of a vacation house is to provide everyone in the family with a place to enjoy doing what they want to do. Try not to do things you don't want to do any more than is absolutely necessary.

A vacation house should be a family affair. Each member of the family should be allowed to enjoy himself more or less as he wishes, but each member should also share in the job of running the place. At the start, assign various daily chores to each member of the family. And it helps if these are rotated so each member of the family gets a crack at doing everything—making the beds, cleaning up the kitchen, hauling in firewood, and so forth. The families who seem to get the maximum pleasure out of their vacation houses—regardless of the size or cost—are those who are involved in their homes and in the land and trees and water around them.

INDEX

249